Does PREACHING have a
FUTURE?

A Call to Join the Conversation
2nd Edition

DR. DWIGHT S. RIDDICK, SR.
FOREWORD BY: DR. FRANK A. THOMAS

DOES PREACHING HAVE A FUTURE?
A CALL TO JOIN THE CONVERSATION

iUniverse books may be ordered through booksellers or by contacting:

iUniverse
1663 Liberty Drive
Bloomington, IN 47403
www.iuniverse.com
1-800-Authors (1-800-288-4677)

Scriptures taken from the Holy Bible, King James Version (Authorized Version). First published in 1611. Quoted from the KJV Classic Reference Bible, Copyright © 1983 by The Zondervan Corporation.

Scriptures taken from the New King James Version®. Copyright © 1982 by Thomas Nelson. Used by permission. All rights reserved.

Scripture quotations marked (NLT) are taken from the Holy Bible, New Living Translation, copyright © 1996, 2004, 2007 by Tyndale House Foundation. Used by permission of Tyndale House Publishers, Inc., Carol Stream, Illinois 60188. All rights reserved.

Other scriptures were taken from the New Revised Standard Version Bible, copyright © 1989 the Division of Christian Education of the National Council of the Churches of Christ in the United States of America. Used by permission. All rights reserved.

ISBN: 978-1-4917-6778-8 (sc)
ISBN: 978-1-4917-6777-1 (e)

Library of Congress Control Number: 2015907582

Print information available on the last page.

iUniverse rev. date: 08/04/2015

CONTENTS

DEDICATION

This book has been a long time coming. Over the years, I have had numerous individuals who have encouraged me to write. Much like Paul and Apollos in the Bible, "some have planted and others have watered, but I offer praise unto God who has given the increase."

I would first like to dedicate this book and express special thanks to my wife, Vera, for her love and unyielding support in all of my endeavors. I'm also indebted to my children, Pastor D. Shawrod, Rev. Jennell, Tiffany, and Mitchell for their creativity, fresh ideas, and youthful insights. My daily delight is in my grandchildren, Dwight III (Little D), Amber, Jasmine, Rhyan, and Tyler (Little Mitch). I hope to leave a legacy of which they will all be proud and footsteps in which they will all follow.

I could never express my gratitude enough for my parents, Willie and the late Gertie Mae Riddick, for the foundation they laid that has influenced every area of my life. I am also grateful to the late Deacon Clinton L. Grandy, the late Reverend Dr. James B. Williams Jr., Deacon Henry Nobles, and my in-laws, the late Edward L. and the late Mary Brite for the impact they each have had upon my life and ministry. They would all be so proud of my accomplishments and especially of this--my first published book.

There are so many more people who deserve to be mentioned, but I'm too wise to continue calling names. For all who have contributed in any way to my life, ministry, or these writings, please place your name <u>here</u> and know that I love and thank God for you. Your encouragement, support, and kindness mean more to me than words can adequately express.

Ultimately, this book is dedicated to the men and women of God who proclaim the gospel of Jesus Christ. It is my prayer that they will be blessed and join in the conversation: *Does Preaching Have a Future?*

FOREWORD

It is difficult to write the Foreword to *The Future of Preaching* by
Dwight Riddick without at least taking a brief look at the past history
of preaching in order to set the context as to why this book is so
important and necessary. In 1927, James Weldon Johnson's poetic
renditions of African American folk sermons of the old-time Negro
preacher appeared in his classic, *God's Trombones.*[1] Johnson believed
that the old-time Negro preacher had not been given proper due and
respect. Though the role and power of the old time Negro preacher
had somewhat lessened and changed in the 20th century, Johnson said,
"The Negro today is, perhaps, the most priest-governed group in the
country."[2]

I still believe that comparatively with other groups and ethnicities,
this is still true. Despite the increasing secularism of this post-modern
age, African Americans are still the most priest-governed group in the
nation. Being priest-governed helps partially explain why I also believe
that there is no other group or ethnicity that treasures and values
preaching more than African Americans. Given the span of my travels,
both nationally and internationally, more lovers of preaching might
exist (probably somewhere in Africa from whence African Americans
come, or people of African descent); but, in the America that I know
best, I can say without fear of successful contradiction that African
Americans love preaching more than any other group.

Preaching has meant the most to African American people. It
was preaching that offered hope when it seemed there was no hope
for a captive people. Preaching sustained, uplifted, encouraged,

---

[1] James Weldon Johnson, *God's Trombones* (New York: Penguin Books,
2008), original (New York: Viking Press, 1927).

[2] Ibid., 2.

and empowered an oppressed, enslaved, Jim Crowed, lynched, and despised people. The God revealed in black preaching was our hope. And this is where *The Future of Preaching* locates itself. Each generation must explain, define, and discuss what preaching is in order to insure that this valuable resource bequeathed to us from old time Negro preachers will still maintain its power and relevancy and continue to sustain and empower African American people and others.

In order to insure this relevancy and empowerment, we must heed the call of Dwight Riddick to dialogue. In *The Future of Preaching*, he has laid out with precision, clarity, insight, and wisdom, critical points of discussion that will definitely impact the future of preaching. His purpose in writing this book is to call you into discussion with him and his ideas. As much as in worship, there are leaders who lead, prompt, or call the people to worship, so there are thought leaders who prompt us to discussion and new revelation. Dwight Riddick is a thought leader who calls us into critical discussions to make preaching relevant for the 21st century.

I hope that you will enter into dialogue with him. His ideas about preaching are generative and are based on the 21st century learning model that will guide us into the new future of collaborative discussion leading to cooperative learning, practice, and teaching. The future of preaching is not in the control of any one group of people concerned with the craft of preaching, i.e. pastors, ministers, homiletic professors, seminary students, and lay people. The future of preaching is in the dialogue and conversations about preaching from many and varied perspectives--even beyond the traditional circles of black preaching.

I highly recommend *The Future of Preaching*. Riddick's experience, insight, education in preaching, pastoral experience, and love of the word and people of God are evident. These pages suggest that you are listening to an accomplished practitioner of preaching who is also able to clearly articulate homiletic method and theory. This book is a must-read for all those who love preaching and are ever seeking to increase their effectiveness in the craft, particularly, in light of the 21st century challenges that we face.

With great joy,

Frank A. Thomas
Nettie Sweeney and Hugh Th. Miller
Professor of Homiletics at
Christian Theological Seminary
Indianapolis, Indiana

PREFACE

My Journey as a Preacher

My journey as a preacher has been long and fruitful. It has taken me from wooden platforms around a manual water pump to hundreds of pulpits across the country. Many doors of opportunity have opened to me since I delivered my first sermon. I have stood in pulpits that I had never dreamed of, and I have had the chance to deliver the president's address for the 101st annual gathering of the prestigious Hampton University Ministers' Conference.

As much as my preaching journey has been rewarding, it has also presented many challenges, particularly as there have been shifts in American culture. Things are not the same now as they were when I entered the ministry. The moral values of people have changed. The respect that some once had for the preacher and for those in the ministry has declined. The medium through which people communicate has changed drastically with the advent of the Internet and other social-media vehicles. Many of the cultural shifts have had a significant impact on those who attend their local churches. Even though the world around us has changed so radically, in many ways the church in the world has not kept up with these changes. It is easy to recognize that few things in traditional churches have changed. Many are still doing the same thing, the same way, with little or no thought to its effectiveness. Buildings often look the same way they have always looked. Worship is the same as it has always been. There is a great possibility that preaching has not changed much at all, especially when members of the congregation can predict what the preacher will say next and how the sermon is going to end. I understand that this is not the case in every setting. However, this may be the reality in many places.

Why I Chose to Write This Book

The inspiration to write this book came as a result of my enrollment in a preaching program. I enrolled in the program to reevaluate my preaching in light of the many changes that are taking place in our culture.

It has been my pleasure to serve as senior pastor of Gethsemane Baptist Church for thirty years. Given such a lengthy tenure, I constantly seek to remain fresh and relevant to all areas of leadership, including my preaching. After a total of thirty-eight years of preaching, with the majority of those years preaching to the same congregation, I wondered whether I was indeed still reaching people in the pews. I constantly asked myself whether or not my messages helped them to live better lives. I wanted to know what my preaching should be like now and what preaching should look like in the future. When seeking answers to those and other questions I have about preaching, a few years ago, I came across a doctor of ministry program in preaching in Chicago, Illinois, that piqued my interest. I had already completed master of divinity and doctor of ministry degrees, but I felt the need to do something further regarding preaching. I later enrolled in the ACTS (Association Chicago Theological Schools) program, only to be asked by many why I was taking classes in preaching after so many years as a pastor. I was not able to answer the question clearly at first. I just knew I wanted to reexamine how I was preaching and to ensure its effectiveness.

The application process for the program required me to collect feedback from members of my congregation regarding my preaching. While the feedback was positive, there was one comment that placed the nail in the coffin and affirmed that I had made the right decision by applying to the program. The comment was simple and unassuming: "Your preaching is predictable." I later asked the individual what she meant. Once again, the reply was simple. "We know that every Sunday we are going to get three points and end at the cross." She added that there was nothing wrong with three points; it had just become the norm or expectation.

Although I was aware that things around me were continually changing, and I often led change in my church, I had not changed my preaching style much in nearly thirty-eight years. I had graduated from seminary and even attended preaching seminars and preaching settings from time to time, but not much in my style or method of delivering a sermon had changed. Like most, I sought to improve in the craft of preaching, but I had only perfected doing things the same way rather than doing things better. After many years, the time had finally come to revisit my preaching style and figure out what it should look like going forward.

I found the ACTS preaching program to be insightful, helpful, and thought provoking. As a result of my participation in the program, I have successfully reevaluated my preaching style and made a few changes here and there that have enabled me to better reach those sitting in the pews. The feedback that I have received from members of my congregation is positive and encouraging.

I often wonder how many preachers of the gospel have stopped to ponder and reconsider their preaching. It is my hope that this book will inspire others to seriously reflect on their preaching. Prayerfully, those who read this book will come away asking themselves and others, in light of the changing culture, what measurable and identifiable changes have occurred in their preaching. Moreover, I hope to inspire them to consider what new tools have been added to their preaching toolbox and what those who listen to them preach week after week are saying.

INTRODUCTION

This book is not designed to talk about new tools for preaching as much as it is intended to ignite conversations regarding the future of preaching among pastors, associate ministers, homiletic professors, seminary students, and those concerned with the craft of preaching. Members of congregations may also find this book helpful as the future of preaching might require a collaborative effort between the pulpit and the pew. Preachers may find it fruitful to engage in conversation with members of their congregation and the community regarding their preaching. In addition, members who understand the preacher's task may enhance the effectiveness of his or her preaching by offering honest feedback.

This book will also focus on the future of preaching in terms of its effectiveness in reaching an unchurched population. Congregations that are experiencing a dwindling number of members sitting in the pews and wish to reach those in their community will find it helpful to engage in conversations regarding preaching.

Discussion questions are suggested at the end of each chapter for the reader to ponder. In addition, these questions can be used in a group setting to further the conversation. After reading each chapter, readers may pose questions of their own regarding the author's thoughts or their particular interests.

Each chapter is based upon a biblical reference. It is important that biblical preaching remains biblically centered. The Bible is a timeless book and has much to say about preaching now and preaching in the future. Given the vastness of scripture, this book only scratches the surface of what the Bible has to say about the future of preaching.

Chapter 1 identifies organizations, groups, and agencies that are holding conversations on the future of their institutions. Those who seek to remain relevant and viable will not sit around and allow their organization to fade away. Rather, there will be an exchange of ideas, a search for the best practices, and a quest for the creativity that is needed to remain effective. Neither the church nor the craft of preaching is any different. If preaching is going to remain alive, fresh, and relevant, there must be an exchange of ideas. Conversations about the future of preaching are currently taking place and must continue. Others are invited to join these conversations by creating venues in their own communities of faith for that purpose.

Chapter 2 addresses the question, is preaching dead, or does preaching have a future? This question is being raised by some within the church and by those who have yet to embrace the church and the validity of preaching. While this question may seem absurd, it must be taken seriously in light of the fact that church doors are closing daily. The future of preaching may very well rest upon the success of preaching that was tested in difficult times in the past. What better place for preaching to be tried than in Ezekiel's valley of dry bones and the preacher's personal experiences?

In chapter 3, the preacher is challenged to be open to new ideas and ways of performing the task of preaching. Like the Israelites who became comfortable traveling in familiar territory, the preacher can be trapped in his or her comfort zone. The voice of God that called the Israelites to leave that place of familiarity may also be the voice that speaks to the preacher today. In this chapter, preachers will face the challenge of rethinking their preaching in a way that is different from how they've considered it in the past.

Chapter 4 acknowledges that our present culture places the modern-day preacher in unfamiliar places and uncharted waters. The preacher is encouraged to embrace the shifts that are taking place and to commit to retool or retrain in order to build confidence and develop a strategy to meet the needs of an emerging culture.

Chapter 5 offers a glimpse of what it is like to preach in a shifting culture. It opens the preacher's worldview so he or she can consider expanding their perspective on the gospel message in a way that reaches people-no matter who they are or where they may be located. In this chapter, Jesus and Paul are examples to be considered and emulated.

In chapter 6, preachers are called to think of those that they should seek to reach with their message, especially those who are unchurched. Preachers need to consider how their preaching is designed to reach those who might not have a church or biblical background. How do language, terms, and other nuances contribute or take away from a sermon's effectiveness? What are matters of concern preachers should be aware of when trying to reach those who are not yet ready to embrace the gospel message?

Chapter 7 emphasizes the importance of preachers remaining biblically sound in their preaching. While a preacher must adapt or adjust in many areas of preaching to remain relevant, there is one thing that must not change: sound biblical doctrine. The gospel's message has not changed; only the manner in which it should be presented in order for it to accomplish its mission has changed.

Chapter 8 speaks to the need to reshape preaching for a generation that may be different from that of the preacher. Churches today are often multigenerational. Given this information, the preacher must wrestle with how his or her preaching is designed to reach each generation that sits in the pews. In addition, the preacher must take into consideration other dynamics that are evident in the community.

The many opportunities and venues that are available to the modern-day preacher are discussed in chapter 9. To secure the future of preaching, the preacher must get acquainted with technology and the various platforms that make preaching mobile. Though we still expect people to gather in a church and sit in the pews, preaching in the future may very well challenge the preacher to reclaim the Great Commission by taking the gospel to the other places where people live, work, and assemble.

In the conclusion of the book, chapter 10, ideas about the future of preaching are discussed. Preaching has met with challenging times before, and it has survived every challenge and overcome every obstacle. The preacher is encouraged to continue preaching with boldness and confidence. Those who preach the gospel trust that when they offer their best, the Holy Spirit does the rest.

CHAPTER ONE

JOIN THE CONVERSATION AROUND THE FUTURE OF PREACHING

Dialogue is a vital threshold through which the Unthinkable crosses over to the Possible generating hope for those involved.

—Laura Chasin

Living in a Changing World

The world has changed in so many different ways since I was called to the ministry in 1977. How those who sit in our pews live, do business, work, and worship is also quite different. In the late '70s, our nation witnessed the launch of Star Wars, a world full of imagination and science fiction. Today, many things like Star Wars, which was the product of the imagination, are now reality. Many of the things that had only been imagined have now found their way into our everyday lives. Through innovation and technology, dreams and visions have become real. This is the day of the Internet, touch screens, iPhones, Droids, iPads, e-mail, Facebook and Twitter. The list goes on. The emergence of these devices and other electronic tools has drastically changed how people provide and process information. Few things function today as they did thirty years ago. Strangely enough, the changes that have occurred are here to stay, and other changes are showing up daily.

Knowing that these changes are occurring, the twenty-first century church and its preachers cannot sit around and wait for things to return to the way they were. The world is on a fast track into the future. Rick Bundschuh says: "Changes in culture that used to take decades or even centuries to happen now spring upon us in microseconds."[3] This is no longer our grandparents' world. It's a new day, and by the time we get used to one thing, something else appears on the horizon. The changes that we now see and experience are happening in every arena and area of life.

The business world recognizes that times have changed. Leaders in Corporate America recognize the shift from modern to the postmodern. Even businesses are being redesigned along postmodern lines. Companies are turning away from hierarchical structures, with

---

[3] Rick Bundschuh, *Don't Rock the Boat: Capsize It* (Colorado Springs: NavPress, 2005), 15.

their clear line of authority and rationalized central planning. Unity, objective organization, and clear-cut authority are modernist values. "Instead, companies decentralize, 'empowering' their employees to make decisions as a part of quality-control groups. Thus, the postmodern values of diversity, the rejection of authority, and the emphasis upon group invades what one might think would be the last bastion of conservatism, the business world."[4]

Veith's comments suggest that even the business world recognizes the changes in the culture and is thinking about the future.

Look Who's Talking About the Future

As conversations about the changing future are taking place, a term that is often used to describe the future is *forward*. Framing issues and discussing ways of *going forward* has become a hot topic in every boardroom. It is on the mind of every CEO or executive of a Fortune 500 company, and a part of conversations of everyone who is concerned about the future of their workplace or vocation. *Forward* has become one of the buzzwords of the new millennium.

Mark Seacombe, deputy production editor of the Observer, sees the phrase "going forward" as an abuse of the English language. He calls it a new development in "corporate doublespeak." While in his mind the use of this phrase is a gross violation of the English language, nonetheless, he admits: "that it has become popularized and widely accepted by the likes of President Barack Obama, David Cameron, film stars, advertising people, and even national newspaper editors. While it may have started in corporate America, "going forward" has

---

[4] Gene Edward Veith Jr., *Post Modern Times: A Christian Guide to Contemporary Thought and Culture* (Wheaton, IL: Crossway Books, 1984), 177.

now penetrated every area of British life. It even came from the mouth of the multilingual Emily Maitlis on Newsnight."[5]

A myriad of synonyms for *forwardness* are being discussed in various circles. For example, "Way Forward" was the title coined by Ford Motor Company upon the arrival of its new CEO, Mark Fields, for its news campaign in early 2006. Like many American auto manufacturers, Ford Motor Company's survival was threatened by changes that were occurring in the auto industry. The Way Forward campaign aimed to refocus the company's business model and thereby lifting it from the ruins of financial failure and repositioning Ford to compete in a competitive global market.

Tim A. Flanagan and John S. Lybarger authored a book entitled Leading Forward: Successful Public Leadership Amidst Complexity, Chaos and Change. Their insightful work joins a plethora of writings addressing shifts in leadership and leadership waves of the future. "Leading Forward" is also a conversation that is being led by Kevin W. Mannoia in his book, Leading Forward: Church 2K.

The term Way Forward is certainly a hot topic when it comes to education. Education is tightly linked to the future of our nation.

"Way Forward" has even made its way into the game industry as a game company includes the phrase in its name. For the last two decades, Way Forward Technologies, Inc. has manufactured games for electronic devices such as Nintendo, PlayStation, and Xbox. Electronic games have changed the way both children and adults are entertained. These games are a long way from the games on which many baby boomers were reared. Undoubtedly, as times goes on, Way Forward Technologies, Inc. and other companies like it will be a game changer in our world.

---

[5] Mark Seacombe, "Going Forward let's consign this insane phrase to history," *Observer*, August 30, 2011, accessed February 17, 2015, http://www.theguardian.com/media/mind-your-language/2011/aug/30/mind-your-language-going-forward.

Clearly, forwardness is not a game. It is a reality with which we must reckon. Of course, all conversations regarding forwardness may not use that exact word. In conversations that address an organization's focus on its future, other words or phrases may be used such as innovation, engineering, and technology. Planning and thinking about the future has captured the attention of almost every discipline. Perhaps the terms future and postmodern are those most commonly used when it comes to matters of forwardness in preaching circles. When I refer to the postmodern world, I use the definition given by Gene Edward Veith Jr. Veith says, "the term 'postmodern' primarily refers to time rather than to a distinct ideology."[6]

Conversations Around Preaching Forward

The discipline of preaching has not been exempt from this discussion—and rightly so. As shifts in almost every area of life are taking place, it is incumbent upon those who practice the craft of preaching to think about the future of preaching and to engage in conversations about it. Failure to think about the future and to engage in those conversations could be tragic. Those who fail to do so may one day discover that they have been left behind. The future of preaching is a conversation that must take place among all who teach or practice the craft. Thankfully, the conversation has begun, and prayerfully it will continue.

Conversations concerning the future of preaching are taking place among both scholars and practitioners. Michael Duduit, who edited a book entitled *Conversations on Preaching*, states in his introduction: "One of the things preachers most enjoy doing is talking preaching with their counterparts."[7] In as much as preachers enjoy talking preaching,

---

[6] Veith, *Post Modern Times*, 19.

[7] Michael Dudiut, ed., *Conversations on Preaching* (Nashville: Salem Publishing, 2011), Kindle edition, loc 22.

we must make sure that the content of the conversation on preaching addresses the future of preaching.

The future of preaching was part of a conversation at the Festival of the Homiletics as early as 2012. The Festival of the Homiletics is a premier conference for preachers, who gather to preach and then lecture on what they seek to accomplish in their preaching. In a 2012 edition of *Patheos* magazine, Tony Jones recalled his conversation about the future of preaching with a colleague as they were sitting in a hotel lobby waiting to go on stage at the Festival of the Homiletics. When Jones and his colleague were ready to present, he acknowledged that few had yet to enter the conversation on the future of preaching. He believed that 99 percent of those who stand to preach on Sundays are continuing with business as usual, without considering cultural shifts that are taking place around them. If Jones's calculation is anywhere near accurate, then the number of those who are preaching week after week without considering how their preaching fits into the future is staggering.

> 99 percent of those who would stand to preach on Sundays are continuing with business as usual without considering cultural shifts that are taking place around them.

Other authors have published insightful and thoughtful materials on the future of preaching. For example, Geoffrey Stevenson edited a book with a broad range of contributors entitled *The Future of Preaching*. Stevenson, who holds a PhD in homiletics, joins those from various denominations, regions, and backgrounds in these conversations. Stevenson and the other contributors cover a broad range of topics that must be discussed and taken into consideration when it comes to the future of preaching or what could be called forward-looking biblical preaching. Their discussion is divided into three sections: contexts, practices, and people.

Graham MacPherson Johnston has presented his thoughts on the future of preaching in his book, *Preaching to a Postmodern World: A Guide to Reaching Twenty-First Century Listeners.* Johnston has done an exceptional job helping his readers understand postmodernity, its obstacles, and its opportunities. According to Johnston, one of the challenges of preaching in this climate is that our message is aimed at a moving target. One of the reasons the discussion about the future is important is that "Our congregation gathers each Sunday and nods at the appropriate spots in the sermon, but in their hearts many parishioners hold deep-seated beliefs and values more in keeping with a postmodern worldview than with a biblical one."[8] As a result, the preaching cannot continue as it has in the past but must be reexamined.

Other Sources Regarding the Future of Preaching

In addition to books on the future of preaching the Internet is loaded with articles and blogs on the subject. One such site is preaching.org, where tons of blogs are posted on a regular basis. This a good place to join the conversation as homiletic professors and practitioners share their ideas, thoughts, and insights on the subject.

In an August 2014 blog, Kenton Anderson suggested that there is a distinction between the future of homiletics and the future of preaching. In his mind, homiletics addresses ways to equip and empower a preacher to better prepare his or her sermons, while preaching is the delivering of the sermon. After making the distinction, he discussed the future of preaching as a return to biblical models in which the message is conveyed through the use of images, pictures, and metaphors, as well as teaching.

---

[8] Graham MacPherson Johnston, *Preaching to a Postmodern World: A Guide to Reaching Twenty-First Century Listeners* (Grand Rapids, MI: Baker Books, 2001), 15.

Today we hear a lot of hard-core exegetical and theological preaching and for that I am grateful. However, there is a needed to return to biblical rootedness and a deeper approach to the word of God. I would like to think that the future, then, could retain this depth while seeking for broader and more integrated expressions of these truths.[9]

Taking into consideration Anderson's thoughts, the conversation about the future of preaching does not mean that the future of preaching must stop with consideration of innovations or creativity; but, rather, it must include a rediscovery of biblical preaching. Certainly today's preachers are not the first to ponder the future of preaching. Conversations regarding preaching must include the work of those who have gone before us as well as those who come after us. Surely we can learn valuable lessons from the past as preachers then also had a challenging future to meet.

William H. Willimon authored a wonderful book entitled *Conversations with Barth on Preaching.* As Willimon understands Barth, he asserts that preaching is always futuristic. "In preaching, we are moving people, little by little, Sunday by Sunday, toward new and otherwise unavailable descriptions of reality."[10]

An additional voice that might be considered in the conversation is that of Fred Craddock. In the book *Conversations on Preaching,* Craddock expressed his concern with what he thought would be an extreme shift in healthy preaching. The shift, as he saw it, was of more exegetical work in the pulpit. He saw preachers opening the Bible, reading verses, and then talking about them. Craddock does not speak as

---

[9] Kenton Anderson, "The Future of Preaching," August 13, 2014, accessed January 25, 2015, http://www.preaching.org/futureofhomiletics/.

[10] William H. Willimon, *Conversations with Barth on Preaching* (Nashville: Abingdon Press, 2006), 115.

much about where he sees preaching going in the future as much as he articulates his concern about how to influence the direction of preaching. "I think, I hope in the future there will be an increase in the dealing with biblical content in the sermon. Some people will find that antiquated or quaint, but the fact of the matter is we live out of the reservoir of the well of the scripture."[11] Craddock's comments suggest that those of old should seek to shape the future of preaching rather than allow the future of preaching to take on shape at will. Those who preach now must ask if they are giving shape to preaching for the future or if they are allowing the future of preaching to go off like a runaway car with an uncertain destination. Though Craddock offers his hopes for the future of preaching, his prediction is "we're going to have more of the ministers as a teaching preacher in the future,"[12] which in his mind is not all bad. While Craddock has his own thoughts about what the future of preaching should look like, at least he is thinking and talking about that future.

James Earl Massey suggests that "preaching as God intended it will never lose its power nor its reason for being. Humans are concerned with the shift with every generation, but God's means of addressing human need will never change."[13] Massey acknowledged that God has always moved in history, and offers a path that must be followed if the preacher is to remain relevant. According to Massey, "preachers must follow God's mandate as given through the apostle Paul, 'Preach the Word, in season and out of season."[14]

Frank Harrington believes there will be an era of renewal in preaching. Harrington expresses the need for relevant terminology in preaching as well as time for preparation, as the minister cannot rely upon what he or she did in previous years. Harrington says, "We

---

[11] Duduit, *Conversations on Preaching*, loc 1112.

[12] Ibid.

[13] Ibid., loc 1027.

[14] Ibid.,

must constantly be digging and grappling with the central questions, because that's what causes us to grow and in our growth we can help our people grow."[15]

Dr. Gardner C. Taylor spoke about the future of preaching as early as 1994. He has seen how religious life drained from American life since his arrival in New York, yet he understands clearly the role of the preacher and preaching in such a culture. He said: preachers are not to scorn the culture: there are notable and wonderful things about it. They are to realize that culture is human, temporal, passing. We are to address our culture as a part of it and yet not a part of it, and to address it with the kind of authority nor arrogance that comes to one who believes that he or she is an emissary of a kingdom that will outlast all kingdoms.[16]

Certainly, those cited above are only a few who are engaged in the conversation about the future of preaching. However, the voices that are being heard all over the world are not the only voices that should be heard. Each preacher should add his or her voice and join the conversation. In the same way that preachers proclaim what they believe they have been given to proclaim about the word of God, they should also speak up and speak out concerning their views of the future of preaching. Every voice is important in this regard. According to Proverbs 27:17 (KJV), "Iron sharpens iron; and one person sharpens the wits of another." Those who are willing to add their voice to the conversation can only help to sharpen others. No one person has the answer to the best style or nature of preaching in the future. In the word of the Apostle Paul in 1 Corinthians 13:12 (KJV), "For now we see through a glass, darkly …" However, if we continue to look and share with each other, it will become clear.

---

[15] Ibid.

[16] Ibid., loc 871.

Questions for Discussion and Reflection:

1. Who do you know that's facilitating conversations around the future of preaching?

2. What conversations about preaching have you been engaged in in the last six months?

3. With whom have you shared those conversations?

4. Do you feel it is necessary to continue the conversation regarding the future of preaching?

5. Do you agree with Jones that 99 percent of those who would stand to preach on Sundays are continuing with business as usual without considering cultural shifts that are taking place around them? Why or Why not?

CHAPTER TWO

PREACHING THAT IS TRIED AND PROVEN

So I prophesied as I had been commanded; and as I prophesied, suddenly there was a noise, a rattling, and the bones came together, bone to its bone. 8 I looked, and there were sinews on them, and flesh had come upon them, and skin had covered them; but there was no breath in them.

—Ezekiel 37:7–8 NRSV

Does Preaching Have a Future?

The title of an article I recently saw on the homepage of an electronic magazine arrested my attention and probed the depths of my soul. It had the audacity to raise a question that was both personally offensive and earth-shattering. Without question, the title, phrased as a question, was designed to be an attention getter, and it certainly accomplished its goal. The inquiry was quite blunt, bold, and boastful: "Is Preaching Dead?" I supposed the article was intended to address or measure the effectiveness of twenty-first century preaching; but, without hesitation, I answered the question that had pierced my soul and blurted out, "No, preaching is not dead." However, glancing down the page, I was compelled to wrestle with the question. I was forced to grapple with the article because it stated that one of the common reasons given for declining church attendance in America is the preaching. According to the article, there is a direct link between the life of a church and the life of preaching.

> Four thousand churches in America close their doors each year.

I am aware that there are those who say church attendance in America is on a steady decline. It is also said that nearly four thousand churches in America close their doors each year. While many reading this book have not had to close the doors to their church, most have seen drastic changes in the church over the past decade. This includes a decline in the number of people who show up for Sunday worship. Are we still preaching to the same crowd Sunday after Sunday? Are we seeing newcomers rushing to the baptismal pool? When newcomers show up, are we merely recycling members who hop from church to church?

Preachers have been preaching that "if any man be in Christ he is a new creature, old things are passed away and behold all things become new." We say that He saves from "the gutter most to the uttermost." Churches print in their bulletins for revival Romans 10:9 (KJV): "That if thou shall confess with thy mouth the Lord Jesus and believe in thine heart that God hath raised Jesus from the dead thou shalt be saved." We do believe that "whosoever shall call on the name of the Lord shall be saved." However, let's be honest. How often are we filling up the baptism pools and singing "Take Me to the Water"? Do we have as many individuals coming down the aisle as we have going out the back door?

Are new member classes running over? Maybe the question posed in that article's title is valid. Just how effective is preaching in the twenty-first century?

Is preaching dead? Maybe another way of looking at that question is by asking: Does preaching have a future? The article suggested that most people do not have the attention span to listen to preaching. "We are told people don't like just hearing someone talk, they are visually-oriented due to the influence of TV and movies. We are told that people don't want a monologue, they want a dialogue, not an information dump but a discussion."[17]

Based upon these and other assertions, we are forced to at least entertain the question—Is preaching dead?—and present an alternate hypothesis.

When I refer to preaching from this point on, it is not just what happens behind a pulpit on a Sunday morning or at some other

Is preaching dead?

time. *Preaching* will refer to the practice and performance of sharing the gospel message that belongs to all who are believers. Pastors,

---

preachers, and people in the pews are to share the good news of Jesus Christ in the "hedges and the highways" as well as on the stately stages of sanctuaries.

A Place to Test Preaching

One of the ways to test whether or not preaching is dead, or if preaching has a future, is to apply it to dead situations and observe its impact and effectiveness when it is properly proclaimed, spiritually saturated, and culturally relevant.

Indeed, this seems to have been the modus operandi employed in Ezekiel 37. The prevailing question posed in the text is, can these bones live? I submit to you that this is not the only question of the text. There are also such questions as: Can preaching bring about positive transformation in the lives of hopeless people and in hopeless cases during changing times?

Cast in the crucible of the ancient text is an utterly hopeless situation. Sadly, the hopelessness evident in the text is not consigned solely to that early culture. It has spilled over into the culture of our day and time. Therefore, if preaching was tried and proven then, in the laboratory of the valley of dry bones, maybe it should also be tried and proven in today's valley of despair.

Hopelessness is seen all over this text. Peek into Ezekiel's vision: in a large valley or vast field, a vicious battle had been fought. The valley is full of bones, a great many bones, hundreds of thousands of bones. The text itself gives commentary on these bones, saying "these bones are the whole house of Israel" Ezekiel 37:11a (KJV). These bones characterize the ten Northern tribes captured and exiled by Assyria in 722 BC, as well as the kingdom of Judah, exiled to Babylon some 135 years later. The entire house of Israel is like a valley full of bones. Its condition is like the church in Sardis that Jesus identified as dead, although it had a reputation for being alive. These bones are dry; they are "very dry" (verse 2b). The death of the house of Israel was not only a recent occurrence. This death had a long history. The bones had been out in the blistering sun for a long time, and all the marrow and life had been drained from them. The dry bones were broken, disjointed, disfigured, dismembered, and scattered all over the valley; and they were not just human skeletons. This is a picture of utter hopelessness and desolation. The people of Israel felt this way about themselves—hopeless, lifeless. In addition, that's how God judged them as hopeless. The questions become pressing: Is there not any hope for them? Is any revival out of the question?

How many have felt hopeless and could not see their situation turning around? How many have been at such a place in their life or ministry where they felt it was over, and nothing about their condition could ever be revived? How many times in life has it seemed impossible to get through difficulties? Many people who sit in the pews Sunday after Sunday feel defeated in some part of their lives with no prospect of things getting better. Israel at that time was a nation of people who were in deep despair.

Ezekiel, living in Babylon, records the lament of an exiled people: "We have become old, dry bones—all hope is gone. Our nation is finished" Ezekiel 37:11 (TNLT). Bones are a vivid image and a relatively common metaphor. Living bones represent life and vibrancy, but bones that lie in the dust are crushed and broken. Therefore, these dry bones were hopeless and powerless.

When people find themselves in a hopeless situation, does that mean that all hope is lost? Can revival still come; and if so, by what means?

Preaching That Is Proven

Interestingly, in this text we see that before the Israelites' hopelessness could be addressed, it first had to be revealed and then personally experienced. God did not send Ezekiel an e-mail informing him that Israel had lost hope. Nor did Ezekiel get the word on Facebook,

Instagram, Twitter, or through some other media source. No, God caused him to be immersed right smack in the context. He canceled Ezekiel's existential position and gave him firsthand experience of the situation and, thereby, provided a full-color illustration of what the people were going through.

Ezekiel said "that the hand of the Lord was upon me"; that it lifted him from his present place of comfort and carried him in spirit to the place of the Israelites' discomfort, setting him down in their midst. Before the prophet could try his preaching out on others, he had to experience what the conditions were like for parched, dry bones.

Before one can answer the question if preaching is dead or if preaching has a future, one must examine the preacher's sensitivity and sense of relevance to the place where he or she is in order to test the authenticity and impact of preaching.

Understand that revival is always preceded by a desperate condition. Before hope can be renewed and restored, there must be an awareness of the hopelessness of the situation. The gospel that is preached and saves lives is a wonderful illustration of this truth. God did not remain at a distance to bring about salvation and restoration. There was, instead, an incarnational event. Jesus humbled himself, taking on the form of a servant. "And the Word was made flesh, and dwelt among us, (and we beheld his glory, the glory as of the only begotten of the Father) full of grace and truth." John 1:14 (KJV)

One wonders whether the modern-day preacher and churchgoer are too far removed from the hopelessness that prevails in our culture today.

- Has our luxurious lifestyle caused us to lose awareness of those to whom we are to give hope?
- Has our learning created a chasm between us and those we are called to reach with the message of optimism and expectation?

- Has our easy life separated us from the task and toil of our assignment, causing us to vacate the valley to which we have been called?
- Have we seen what hopelessness looks like lately?
- Do we know what hopelessness feels like?
- Have we smelled the unpleasant odor of hopelessness in the dark alleys of our own experiences?
- Have we heard the agonizing crying of hopelessness?
- Can we taste the bitter gall of hopelessness of those who sit at the table of disappointment and sorrow?

Trust me, hopelessness is all around us.

Even though we have the greatest technology the world has ever known, despair is still evident. Even though we have the most sophisticated methods of communication of any society in history, and have access to more modern conveniences than our forebears ever dreamed of, hopelessness rates high on the charts of the human heart.

It seems that our times too are filled with examples of dryness. We often live in barren wastelands. There are wastelands of addictions, failing marriages, dry churches, and personal emptiness.

God's question for Ezekiel then is also addressed to us now. Can these bones live? Can addicts, destroyed by the powerlessness of their compulsions, live again? Can marriages, in which love has been extinguished by selfishness and broken promises, live again? Can churches devastated by scandal, rendered comatose by traditionalism, or killed by unbelief live again?

> God's question for Ezekiel then is also addressed to us now.

Maybe, in order to test the hypothesis of the modern culture, that the church and preaching are either on a ventilator or have already expired, we will have to sit where they sit. Maybe some will have to sit on sidewalks in front of walls that have been decorated with the graffiti of the gangs that claim the street corners they did not purchase or pay taxes to maintain.

Maybe we have to stand in some dark alley and watch addicts pump poison into their veins and take a life that they do not have the power to give back.

Maybe we have to hold the hand of a single mother who is sobbing because she doesn't know where she'll get the funds to pay her rent, put food on the table, or put clothes on her children's backs.

Maybe some will have to stand in lines with the unemployed, underemployed, and refused to be employed, and feel with them the pain of rejection when they hear those disappointing words—"Sorry," "no openings," "unqualified."

Maybe we will have to go to the classrooms of a generation that has yet to frequent our sanctuary, read our Bible, and believe in our God, but who are looking for solutions to the problems of their lives.

The list could go on.

- What do hopelessness and despair look like in your city?
- What does it feel like in the neighborhood where your church is planted?
- How clear is it on the road that you travel?

Preaching and the Power of God

The valley of the dry bones was such a sight that when God asked Ezekiel if the bones could live, his response was that this has got to be a God thing.

- If there was any hope for these bones, it could not come from the outside.
- If there was any restoration that could take place, it would not be by human effort.

- If there was any ray of hope, it had to come from on high.
- If there were any prospect of life returning to this valley, then God was the only one who knew that and was the only one who could make it happen.

Is this not the assignment of the preacher? Preachers have been called, anointed, appointed, ordained, and trained to declare hope to a hopeless generation. No matter the times in which we live, the preaching should speak to dead situations and declare that they can live again.

That is what the preacher has been sent to do. He or she must speak to deaf ears, touch lifeless situations, and lead those who are blind to the place of sight.

Jesus recited the prophet Isaiah, declaring, "the Spirit of the Lord is upon me, because he has anointed me to bring good news to the poor. He has sent me to proclaim release to the captives and recovery of sight to the blind, to let the oppressed go free."[18]

Preaching Hope

The prophet Ezekiel does not sit down and observe, nor does he walk around and critique the setting. He does not use his time to criticize the culture. He does not pass judgment on the bones, nor does he blame them for being in the condition that they are in. He does not try to separate himself from them or inoculate himself from the possibility of being infected or affected by them.

Rather, he walks into the middle of the horror scene and ponders their prospects for their future. He sees these bones in their present state and then receives a vision of what they can become. He could never get that vision on his own, but he has an encounter with God

---

[18] Luke 4:18 (KJV)

that allows him to see what God sees. He comes to grips with the fact that if preached to, these dry bones can live again.

Therefore, his assignment is to declare unto the bones what God has showed him about their future. He does not have to fuss with the bones. He does not have to fight with the bones. He does not have to call a business meeting and ask the bones to vote on what they want to become. All he has to do is tell the bones what God said about their future.

Truthfully, that's all a preacher is charged to do—preach the message of hope and the message of healing. That is the medicine that will work the miracle of restoring life to dry bones. That is what our world needs today, and that is what the world will need tomorrow.

In a time of sequestration, frustration, and government shutdowns; in a season of gender-identity crisis; during times of strange and strangling diseases; in a period of spiritual and moral decay, our world needs the message of hope and a vision of how God can deliver us out of our predicaments. The preacher is the only one with that message.

- Who else is preaching hope? Who else has been entrusted with the message of the good news?
- Who else has been charged to go into a valley of dry bones and declare, thus saith the Lord?
- God has chosen the "foolishness of preaching" to save a dying world. The prophet will have to test this message and its effectiveness in a dry and dead situation. But before he can test it on others, he must first see if it works for him.

Preacher, do You Believe?

Before God sent Ezekiel with the message of hope, He asked him this question: "Son of man, can these bones live?"

Ezekiel had to believe the message himself before he could declare it to others. If he believed that the bones could live, chances are they would. On the other hand, if he did not believe the bones could live, then his message to them would be useless.

Does the preacher believe that his or her message can be effective going forward? If the preacher believes that preaching can be effective and has a future, it will. However, if preachers are skeptical about the future of preaching and its effectiveness, then preaching as we know it will die. Every believer must wrestle with these and other probing questions:

- Can these bones live?
- Can your church grow?
- Can you blossom right where you are?
- Can your community be turned around?
- Can the economy be restored?
- Will God take care of you?
- Can your ministry help bring about a change in the lives of others?

Richard Sibbes, one of the great old Puritan preachers of Cambridge, who died in 1635, wrote a whole book on Psalm 42:5. Sibbes was called "the sweet dropper" because of how much confidence and joy his sermons delivered. He called his book *The Soul's Conflict with Itsel,* because in Psalm 42:5 that is exactly what you have—the soul arguing with itself, preaching to itself. "Why are you cast down, O my soul and why are you disquieted within me? Hope in God!"

Hope in God does not come naturally for sinners like us. We must preach it to ourselves, and preach it diligently and forcefully, or we will give way to a downcast and disquieted spirit.

That great warrior of the Bible, David, found himself in deep despair. Still, he encouraged himself in the Lord. The preacher must first test his sermon on himself.

- If the preacher's gospel does not encourage the preacher, if it does not bring about a change in his life and circumstances, then there is a great possibility it will not work for anyone else.
- If during the times of the preacher's own struggles and dry moments, he or she can still proclaim the gospel message, then preaching may still be alive.
- When the preacher comes to the end of his or her rope; when his enemies have come upon him; when he comes to the pulpit knowing how people have treated him, talked about him, and worked against him, he can declare that "my hope is built on nothing less than Jesus' blood and His righteousness. I dare not trust the sweetest frame, but wholly lean on Jesus' name. On Christ the solid rock I stand all other ground is sinking sand."[19]

When that can happen, then I think you are on to something. Son of man, do you think that these bones can live?

Try Preaching to the Bones

- Prophesy to them, preach to them, proclaim the word to them. "I charge thee therefore before God, and the Lord Jesus Christ, who shall judge the quick and the dead at his appearing and his kingdom, Preach the word: be instant in season, out of season" (2 Timothy 4:2 KJV).
- Preach the word because "how then shall they call on him in whom they have not believed? And how shall they believe in him of whom they have not heard? And how shall they hear without a preacher?" (Romans 10:14 KJV).

---

[19] The Solid Rocks Lyrics, *The Solid Rock,* 2015. http://library. timelesstruths.org/music/The_Solid_Rock/

- What should be the introduction to the sermon? Tell them to hear the word of the Lord, because "faith cometh by hearing, and hearing by the word of God" (Romans 10:17 KJV).
- What is your antithesis? Your bones are dry.
- What is your thesis? Dead, dry bones can live again? "Jesus said unto her, I am the resurrection and the life: he that believeth in me, though he were dead, yet shall he live" (John 11:25 KJV).
- What is your first point? God "will cause breath to enter into you, and ye shall live" (Ezekiel 37:5 KJV).
- What is your second point? God "will lay sinews upon you, and will bring up flesh upon you, and cover you with skin" (Ezekiel 37:6 KJV).
- What is your third point? God will breathe in you, and ye shall live: and know that He is God.
- What is the conclusion of the sermon? God will stand you on your feet and cause you to become a mighty army again.

So, the Prophet said, I just preached as I was commanded.

By the end of point number one, the bones shouted Amen. In Ezekiel 35:7, there is a noise in the crowd. By the end of point number two, the noise gets louder and the people start clapping. The text states that there is a shaking. By the end of point three, the noise gets even louder, and the people start shouting. As the text says, the bones come together.

Preaching Still Works

From the experience of Ezekiel, it appears that preaching works. Is preaching dead? Does preaching have a future? Based on the evidence in my own life and based on the evidence of the text of Ezekiel 35, it works and it has a future.

A few years ago, I was diagnosed with cancer. It happened during the Hampton University's Ministers' Conference. I had to miss one Friday morning at the conference because I was scheduled for surgery. The doctors needed to do a biopsy to determine if their speculation was true. It was. When I was told that I had cancer, I immediately turned to the word of God, and for several weeks I preached to myself on divine healing. I developed a sermon series called, "Fight for Your Healing." I am alive today and cancer free. Ask me: does preaching work? You better believe it works! Does preaching have a future? You bet it does.

When Ezekiel finished preaching, Ezekiel 37:10 (KJV) says: "So I prophesied as he commanded me, and the breath came into them, and they lived, and stood up upon their feet, an exceeding great army." Does preaching work? You better believe it works.

The resurrected Christ is one more witness. According to 1 Peter 3:19 (KJV), "By which also he went and preached unto the spirits in prison;" 1 Peter 4:6 (KJV) states, "For this cause was the gospel preached also to them that are dead, that they might be judged according to men in the flesh, but live according to God in the spirit." Matthew 27:53 (KJV) "And the graves were opened; and many bodies of the saints which slept arose, and came out of the graves after his resurrection, and went into the holy city, and appeared unto many."

I've wondered why Jesus would go to hell and preach. Could it be that if preaching works in hell, it can work anywhere? When preaching has been tested, tried, and proven, then preaching will transcend every generation who will still need to hear the preaching of the gospel. The question may be, to whom shall we preach in a postmodern world?

In the next chapter I will address the preaching that must be prepared to enter the future, if it will take on the postmodern world.

Questions for Discussion and Reflection:

1. In what places has your preaching been tested?
2. How would you describe the scenes of hopelessness around you?
3. What impact has the preaching of others had in your life?
4. What impact has your own preaching had in your life?
5. How have you seen preaching change hopeless situations?

CHAPTER THREE

CROSSING THE BROOK

"Now then, proceed to cross over the Wadi Zered." So we crossed over the Wadi Zered.

—Deuteronomy 2:13 NRSV

Embracing the future is a dominant theme that runs throughout scripture. It is certainly the theme that defines the journey of the Israelites toward their God-given destiny. In Deuteronomy 2, God spoke to his chosen prophet and leader, Moses, and instructed him to move forward. Moses had been leading the people around in a circle. Without question, he and the people of Israel were enjoying a mountaintop experience. They had completed their exodus from Egypt, escaping the oppression of the Egyptians and miraculously evading their enemy as they crossed the Red Sea. Their journey took them to Mount Seir. "Mount Seir is the original name of the mountain range extending along the east side of the valley of Arabah, from the Dead Sea to the Elanitic, Gulf."[20] Together, both the people and their leader were enjoying their experience on the mountain. The people were not only enjoying it, they had become content on the mountain. Time and time again, they circled the mountain, traveling the same landscape, observing the same scenes, experiencing the same things, hearing the same sounds, and smelling the same odors. If ever there was a case where familiarity bred contentment, this was it.

In addition to their familiarity with the mountain, the people's contentment grew because they were continually blessed and their needs were met. Perhaps some wondered why they should bother a good thing. Why upset the apple cart? If it's not broken, then don't fix it. However, God's will for them was greater than the blessing in the mountain. He had a larger purpose for their journey, and did not want them to grow content and satisfied where they were.

So, God appears to Moses and instructs him to speak to the people and tell them they have circled this mountain long enough and to turn and cross the Brook Zered.

When God said this to Moses, he was telling Moses to go forward. Moses was to lead the people ahead and to a place they had not seen before. Crossing the brook and moving forward would present new

---

[20] William Smith, *Smith's Bible Dictionary,* http://ww42.biblestudy.com/.

challenges for the Israelites. They would have to leave the familiar, face the unfamiliar, and trust God as they journeyed to a place that was completely foreign. They would see new places, travel along new territories, explore new terrain, and even encounter new enemies.

When Change Is Necessary

It was necessary for the Israelites to cross the brook if they were to experience God's best. They had not been delivered from Egypt just to remain in the same place. The blessing that God had in store for them was still ahead.

The brook they had to cross represented a barrier that kept them from the destiny God had in store for them. Perhaps one of the reasons they circled the mountain so many times was because of that brook. Could they have seen the brook as a challenge or an obstacle they had to overcome? Rather than take on the challenge or seize the opportunity, they remained in the place of familiarity.

A brook by definition is a small, shallow stream of water. Though this brook was small, it had major implications for the Israelites. It suggested that the present obstacle was nothing in comparison to what God had already done for them. The Brook Zered was minute in comparison to the Red Sea. When they crossed the Red Sea, God had to perform a miracle. He sent strong winds to create a path through the sea so that they could cross over. The brook did not require such a miracle; it only required obedience. They could walk across it without the threat of enemies chasing them, waters drowning them, or any other life-threatening situations.

Crossing the brook would also lead to overcoming other barriers they would meet as they moved toward their future. The people's willingness to take on small challenges now would prepare them to take on greater challenges in the future. God would use this opportunity to both test them and prepare them.

According to Exodus 13: 21–22, when the Israelites crossed the Red Sea, the visible presence of God was with them. There was a "cloud by day" and a "pillar of fire by night" that either went before them or behind them. This visible manifestation of God in the cloud and the pillar of fire did not require the level of faith that would be required in future challenges. God would use the brook experience to determine whether or not the people trusted him in small things.

God Prepares Us Now for the Future

Crossing the brook would be instrumental in preparing the people to trust God in other matters. Victory and success in small ways increases one's courage to take on greater challenges. The second line in the hymn, "Yield Not to Temptation," says, "Each victory will help you some other to win." Leaving the mountain and crossing the brook would help build the necessary strength in the Israelites to detach from other things and to overcome the challenges that were sure to come.

God's command went beyond leaving the mountain and crossing the brook. It was also a time of transitioning from one generation to another. Nearly forty years had gone by since the people had left Egypt. The soldiers who carried weapons for protection were nearly wiped out. The people who crossed the brook would enter a new place without the former generation. They would no longer be guarded by the warriors they had always known. The instruments and tools that had once offered them security would not accompany them to the other side of the brook. They would be vulnerable to attacks on the other side. Despite this, it was fitting to leave the tools and weapons of the previous generation behind. The new generation that would cross over would face different challenges and obstacles, and thus would need different sets of tools.

In addition, crossing the brook represented Israel leaving its past, experiencing the present, and anticipating the future. They would pass through Moab and head toward the land God had promised them. No longer would they be content to live in the past. No longer would they circle the same mountain. No longer would they live in the old. Their future was calling them to a new place with new challenges but also with great expectations.

God Commands Us to Cross Over

In the same way that the word of God came to Moses, commanding him to leave the mountain of familiarity and cross the brook, those who are in the ministry today are also commanded to cross brooks. The minister is to cross the brook in many areas, even in the preaching of the gospel. The commanding voice of God that speaks to the twenty-first century preacher can be heard loud and clear through the myriad changes in our postmodern world. It is vitally important that those who are preaching the gospel understand these times. As it says in 1 Chronicles 12:32 (KJV): "And of the children of Issachar, which were men that had understanding of the times, to know what Israel ought to do." Every era or generation has its uniqueness and distinctiveness that requires adjustments and realignments. The craft of preaching is no exception. While the message of the gospel must not change, the methods and practices must be reexamined and reengineered for the times.

Preachers who began their preaching career in the modern era and continue to preach must ask if the form and content of their sermons is the same now as it has always been. Have some become so content with their preaching style that, like the people of Israel, they continue to circle the same mountain? Has the style, structure, and content of their preaching experienced little or no change? Have some become a "selfish performer," preaching to a beat that satisfies the preacher without regard to its effectiveness to a new generation? The preacher of today must respond to a new call-the call to cross the brook.

Crossing the Brook Is a Challenge

Crossing this brook presents a great challenge for most and will require the ability to operate at a new level of faith as the preacher stands behind the sacred desk. Preachers must ask themselves if they can trust God with minor shifts in their preaching. Can the preachers who preach to others about the need to abandon old traditions and accept new ways of doing things abandon the familiarity of their own preaching style? Can they accept and adapt to new models and methods of delivering the gospel message?

If the modern-day preacher is going to reach the world in which we all now live, crossing the brook is not only critical to the survival of his or her career, but it is essential to fulfilling his or her God-given calling. I would be the first to admit that it is difficult to depart from the past, break with familiarity, and explore new directions. This is especially true when the past has proven successful and has delivered a person to his or her present place in the ministry. Departing from the past and embracing the unfamiliar may be one of the greatest struggles preachers have to face.

One of the daunting questions that must be addressed is, what new tools has the preacher added to his preaching toolbox lately? When I refer to the preacher's toolbox, I am not speaking of Bibles, new translations, commentaries, or even Bible programs for electronic devices. I'm referring to the various methods a preacher uses when approaching the preaching moment, including different sermon models and various ways of presenting or delivering the message.

Adding new tools to the preacher's toolbox does not suggest that the preacher is not already growing and maturing. It simply means that he or she is better equipped to face an

> Growing in areas of familiarity may not be sufficient to keep the preacher fresh and relevant.

uncertain future. I like to think that we all get better with time. While we are constantly growing and honing our skills, the preacher must seek to grow in new ways too. Simply growing in areas of familiarity may not be sufficient to keep the preacher fresh and relevant. The preacher must be ready to make necessary shifts from time to time and to remain open to possibilities that he or she has not known or experienced.

The Challenge to Rethink Preaching

Preachers must be challenged to rethink preaching. There have been several books and articles on rethinking various areas of the church such as Apostle Jean Saflo's *Rethinking the Church for the 21ˢᵗ Century* and James E. White's *Rethinking the Church: A Challenge to Creative Redesign in an Age of Transition*. Other authors have written on topics such as rethinking evangelism, rethinking the Great Commission, rethinking biblical discipleship, and rethinking your purpose. The list goes on. However, the conversation regarding new approaches to preaching is just now on the horizon. One conversation on the subject has been started by Clayton King, president of Crossroads Ministries. King recently wrote in an article published on the Internet:

> As a pastor and evangelist, I am often asked about preaching in the 21ˢᵗ century. The questions usually take one of the following forms: Does preaching need to sound different to reach a more secular culture? How do pastors connect to non-believers from the pulpit? What are some ways to invite people to respond to the gospel during a sermon? These are not only good questions; they are essential to the future of the church and the eternal destinies of those who have never heard the gospel. To answer these questions, we need to think like missionaries. Most

> of us would agree that a vital part of international missions is preparing those who go to engage those to whom they are sent. Missionaries have to learn as much as they can about the language, the culture, the history and the context of the people they are attempting to reach with the gospel. I encourage preachers in the United States to do the same.[21]

While more preachers are receiving formal training today than ever before, the question must be raised: Does formal training focus more on the past or does it have an eye toward the future? Are homiletics taught in such a way that preachers are trained to sound more like those who have gone before, or are they encouraged to chart new paths for the purpose of reaching a new generation?

In 2011, the Alban Institute published an article entitled "Rethinking Ourselves as Preachers." The article quoted an unnamed preacher who began to rethink his preaching once he noticed the inadequacy of his image of the preacher.

Does formal training focus more on the past or does it have an eye toward the future?

> I had consumed my seminary education voraciously and had gone on reading and teaching in various venues ever since: I had a lot to share! But in the mid-1990s I began to ask whether making the Christian tradition—its ideas about God, its sacred texts, its

---

[21] Clayton King, *"Rethinking Preaching: Whatever It Takes to Make the Gospel Clear,"* Facts & Trends, April 28, 2014, accessed February 2, 2015, factsandtrends.net/2014/04/28/rethinking-preaching-whatever-it-takes-to-make-the-gospel-clear/#.VPSq_PnF-sSo.

liturgical practices—accessible and user-friendly to
my listeners was what I really needed to be doing.[22]

The preacher went on to tell the story of a five-year-old child
who was able to identify an item contained in a replica of a tabernacle
in the church sanctuary. Small children were regularly brought into
the sanctuary to share with the larger congregation lessons they'd
learned in children's church. The five-year-old child volunteered to
come to the front of the congregation and answer questions about the
tabernacles. When the child answered the questions correctly and
returned to her seat, the congregation applauded her. The pastor was
concerned because he knew the majority of his congregation would
not have been able to answer the same questions. He said:

> The culture of the church often makes adults feel
> uncomfortable asking basic questions about things
> they don't understand but feel they should. So the
> child's demonstration became a safe way for adults to
> learn. What was a source of wonder and discovery for
> a five-year-old, however, became mere information
> for most of the congregation. Being better informed
> about the name of the ornate silver vessel inside the
> elaborately carved wooden box made them feel more
> confident about the practices of their religion, but it
> had not necessarily revealed something essential about
> God to them. When the items were first presented
> to them in their dedicated space, the children in the
> atrium had had a chance to wonder aloud about the
> tabernacle and the ciborium and what it all meant

---

[22] Alban Institute, *"Rethinking Ourselves as Preachers,"* Alban Roundtable Blog, November 15, 2011, accessed February 2, 2015, https://alban.org\archive\rethinking-ourselves-as-preachers/.

about God and God's place in their lives. When would the congregation have such an opportunity? It was then that I began to wonder whether my preaching was like the little girl's demonstration of the ciborium without the ensuing reflection and engagement. Was I, in effect, holding up the texts of the Bible week by week to the congregation and simply giving my listeners information about those texts, even if that information was more subtle and complex than the five-year-old's identification of the ciborium? Was I speaking as the seminary-trained "expert" to the "uneducated" laity? Certainly this was no part of my conscious understanding of what I was doing, but I began to question the ways my own education and the ordination process itself had formed me in such a model despite my best intentions.[23]

Here was a preacher who was daring and willing to rethink preaching and reexamine its effectiveness. Those who have received training, formal or informal, might consider continuing education or even retooling. I once asked a group, how many of them would visit a doctor who was still practicing medicine as he had thirty years ago. How many would stick with a physician who still used the same equipment, the same technology, and the same methods that he or she has used for decades? While these methods and models may have been the best available then, advancements and new discoveries had rendered them outdated. Similarly, preaching must be adequate for the times in which we live. The preacher in the twenty-first century must consider new approaches to preaching as well as seek out new insights on preaching. Like Israel, the preacher might have circled this mountain long enough. Is it your time to cross the brook?

---

[23] Ibid.

In the next chapter, I will seek to encourage the preacher to tackle and take on unfamiliar territory. While every preacher is comfortable with what he or she has known in the past, the future will certainly usher them into unknown and uncharted territory. The preacher in the twenty-first century will not be the first to encounter the unfamiliar. Others before us have faced the unfamiliar with faith, fierceness, and fortitude.

Questions for Discussion and Reflection:

1. One of the daunting questions that must be addressed is what new tools has the preacher added to his or her preaching toolbox lately?
2. In your estimation, is the rethinking of preaching critical to your future as a proclaimer of the gospel?
3. To what extent are you willing to trust God to make shifts in your preaching?
4. What do you see as a change that is necessary to the future of preaching?
5. Given the outcome and end result of your preaching, what changes could you make to promote greater effectiveness?

CHAPTER FOUR

FACING THE UNFAMILIAR

Saul clothed David with his armor; he put a bronze helmet on his head and clothed him with a coat of mail. David strapped Saul's sword over the armor, and he tried in vain to walk, for he was not used to them. Then David said to Saul, "I cannot walk with these; for I am not used to them." So David removed them.

—1 Samuel 17:38–39 NRSV

My wife and I enjoy vacationing in Myrtle Beach. When we were first called to serve Gethsemane Baptist Church, we would go to Myrtle Beach almost every summer. As time went on, though, we wanted to see other places and try different things. After several years, we decided to return to our old stomping ground. We did not have to fly or get on a cruise ship for this one. Myrtle Beach was just a six-hour drive from our home. So we packed our bags, got in the SUV, picked up friends, and off we went.

Upon our return home, our son asked us what had been adventurous about the trip, and our honest answer was: the drive.

Quite frankly, when we left home for Myrtle Beach, I thought I knew the way. Years ago, before GPS, we would always go to AAA and get a map outlining our trip. While I still have AAA, I also have GPS in my vehicle. This time, I put the address in my GPS and off we went. For a while, we were on a familiar path. However, as time went on, that heavy female voice on my GPS said, "In one mile, take the exit on the right."

That is not right, I thought. *The GPS is not leading us in the right direction.*

Ignoring the voice of the GPS, I kept on driving. Needless to say, there had been some changes on the highway, and the farther we drove, the more unfamiliar the road became. So much so, we decided to get off and ask someone if we were on the right road. We discovered we should have followed the voice prompt of the GPS. We got back in sync with the GPS—until we mistakenly got off an exit too early. The GPS was kind to us. It automatically rerouted us, and we were on track again. But this time, we were driving down back roads and through neighborhoods. We were no longer on the main highway. We were off the beaten path, and the roads were winding, narrow, and strange. We were in an unfamiliar place. I do not have to tell you how we felt. We were out of control and had to rely totally on the GPS. We felt like strangers, lost, and we were all wondering: *Where is this going to take us?* The more we drove, the deeper our sense of being lost became, and the more we worried. But to our surprise, we got there. It was a different way and from a different direction than what we were familiar with, but we got there.

We have all found ourselves in unfamiliar places. It may not have been while you were on your way to a vacation spot or traveling to some other destination, but we have all had to chart unfamiliar territory.

An Unfamiliar Place

An unfamiliar place. That is what is going on in 1 Samuel 17. A group of people are in an unfamiliar place, the Valley of Elah. Saul, that tall fellow, the first king of Israel, is standing out in front of his soldiers. They are all dressed in their armor, and they are armed and ready for battle. They have chariots driven by stout, strong horses. The expression on their faces says that they mean business. On the opposite side of the valley, at ShoChoh, there's another army, the Philistines. They too are dressed for battle. They have their weapons in hand, and are accompanied by horse-driven war chariots.

As the opposing forces face each other, ready for battle and waiting for the command to attack, through the Philistines' battle line emerges a huge figure, a man of a super human size. He's twice the height of any of the Israelite soldiers, including Saul. Can you imagine someone standing in front of you who is two times as tall as you? It was nearly paralyzing for the Israelites to look at him; and when he opened his mouth, out came this heavy, thunderous voice that caused the ground to tremble. His message was short and simple. He offered a one-on-one competition, and whoever won would defeat the entire army of his opponent.

No one in Saul's army responded. The challenge was announced daily for several days and each time this giant's presence became more threatening than before. Can you imagine being in a fight with someone who was twice your size and so fearsome, the ground shook when he spoke?

Goliath is his name. You know him. We have called this narrative the story of David and Goliath, but I like to think that it is the story of Saul and the Unfamiliar. In my estimation, Goliath's challenge cast Saul and his army into an unfamiliar place. His challenge was far greater than any of them had ever encountered. This was a challenge to fight a battle in a manner they had never fought before. Israel had seen giants before, but not this generation of Israelites. This generation was under the leadership of Saul, and Saul knew nothing of giants.

Warfare was not new to Israel. She had fought battles before. She had won some and lost some. She had faced armies large and small—even armies with horses and chariots. She had been in the valley and she had been on the mountain. However, this was a different kind of battle. Never before had Saul and his army had to fight like this. Never before had they faced someone of this stature, and never before had they been challenged to fight one on one in order for an entire army to be delivered. It was all different now. Goliath was more than his gigantic size. He represented a new era, a new kind of warfare, a new way of doing things. He represented a new dimension and a new world. Goliath and his challenge presented a paradigm shift that put Saul and his army in a strange situation.

Needless to say, they were baffled, they were stunned. They were at a loss for words and direction. Fear set in because they did not know what to do or how to respond. They were paralyzed and couldn't respond. They were suffering from a spiritual generational curse for they saw themselves as their forebears once saw themselves: as grasshoppers in their own eyes. They had reached a point of hopelessness, and felt like it was over for them. As they surveyed their ranks, there was no one with answers or solutions. No one was able to take on Goliath. The challenge was greater than they could handle. They had come face-to-face with the unfamiliar.

In like manner, twenty-first century preachers are prone to find themselves in an unfamiliar place. As already mentioned, the crowds to whom we are called to preach are vastly different. Commitment to anything or anyone is near nonexistent; loyalty is low on the totem pole. Values once held high are vanishing, and the worshippers who show up in our pews desire a certain level of entertainment. People do not appear to be as stable emotionally, financially, socially, or otherwise. Leaders in many churches seem to be missing in action. It is a new day and a new crowd.

Though the preacher faces new challenges in proclaiming the gospel message and in ministry, scripture reminds us: "There hath no temptation taken you but such as is common to man: but God is faithful, who will not suffer you to be tempted above that ye are able; but will with the temptation also make a way to escape, that ye may be able to bear it" (1 Corinthians 10:13 KJV). God has a way to meet every challenge.

Taking on That Which Belongs to God

Saul and his men had approached this battle without faith in God. They were under the mistaken impression that this was their war, their battle, their fight. Because they saw this as their responsibility, they did not see any victory or any deliverance. So it is when we look at our battles as solely *our* battles, our struggles as solely *our* struggles, our challenges as only ours. We too will always see defeat. But this battle did not belong to them, it belonged to God.

The challenges that we face in ministry do not belong to us. Could it be that a major problem in our lives, in our churches, and in our ministries is that we have misplaced ownership? We

> The challenges that we face in ministry do not belong to us.

are claiming what belongs to God. Have we become possessive? Now, it's our church, it's our ministry, and it's our problem! Like Saul and his army, we see our challenges as being larger than our resources because it's ours rather than God's. Therefore, we believe we have to deal with our problems based on who we are and what we have. Saul was a tall man, he had armor that had been made just for him, yet he was no match for Goliath. He had no one in his ranks who was a match for Goliath. As long as he saw the battle as his responsibility, he would never have what it took to defeat Goliath.

So it is with you and me. We are no match for the challenges that we face. We are not smart enough or strong enough. We do not have enough resources. The challenges are too great.

When we take on the problems of life and the ministry as our own, we violate one of the fundamental principles of life. When I was growing up, my mother taught me not to take anything that didn't belong to me. In fact, I used to get my fingers popped when I did. She would tell me that if something did not belong to me, I had no business with it. If I took something that wasn't mine, I had to give it back to the person to whom it belonged and apologize. Some of us may need to apologize to God, and give ourselves as preachers and the ministry of preaching back to him. "But we have this treasure in earthen vessels that the excellency of the power may be of God, and not of us."[24]

When we face the greatest challenges of life, God steps in and reminds us that this is not our fight. After Saul and his men failed to step up to the plate, God sent David. It was no accident that Jesse, David's father, prepared food and told David to go down to the Valley of Elah to check on his brothers. God was in the picture. Preachers must keep God at the forefront of their preaching. God's call to a preacher is what qualifies the preacher to take on the challenge ahead. God knows when we need help, and he knows when we need deliverance from ourselves.

---

[24] 2 Cor. 4:7 (KJV)

The Right Attitude Concerning the Uncertainty of the Future

God knew David had the right attitude and that he could turn the attitudes of others. God knew that David understood the times. He had discernment and he would know how to address the people. David knew the following:

- Goliath was powerful, but he was not all powerful.
- Goliath was mighty, but he was not almighty.
- Goliath was experienced, but he was not eternal.
- Goliath was the champion, but he was not the Alpha and Omega.
- God is big enough to handle his own business.
- The battle was not his, but the Lord's.
- God was looking for a vessel that could be used. That is all God is really looking for, a willing vessel.

David teaches us that the size of the vessel does not matter. He was nowhere near the size of Goliath, but that was not a factor. What really mattered was the size of his God. The size of your church and the size of your ministry are not factors in what God can do. God is just looking for a faithful vessel that he can work through. See, size only matters when we are comparing ourselves to each other. We need to get our eyes off other people's ministry and refocus on what God has commissioned us to do. It is not your size that matters. Sometimes what matters is that you show up when you're supposed to.

Your ability is not a factor when the battle does not belong to you. What really matters is God's ability. Some tried to tell David he was not able. They told him he was not qualified to fight this champion of a giant, but David understood that it was not his ability that mattered. David had history with his God. Bears and lions had attacked his sheep and with his bare hands, he had defeated them through the power of God.

It is not about your degree. Don't get me wrong, you ought to study we need to go to school. But it is not the degree on the wall that gets the victory. Rather, it is the degree of your anointing that matters. It is not how smart you are that gets the job done; it is how much faith you release in God's ability to get the job done through you.

An individual might not have all of the qualifications that the world is looking for; but what the world looks for is one thing, and what God looks for is another. The world looks at the outward appearance of a man; God looks at the heart.

David knew that it was not how well equipped a person is that ultimately makes him successful. Saul wanted to arm David with his armor, and with his sword and shield, but David said those belonged to a different man and a different generation. He instead wanted to use what he had already proved worked for him.

The Right Stuff for the Future

The tools that David had proved worked for him were not the tools of Saul and his men. His tools belonged to his generation. How does this relate to our generation here and now?

For those facing the giant of this generation, it may simply mean that the preacher will have to rise above any fear of facing this new generation. In addition, it may mean that the preacher will have to learn how to use new tools. This is the world

> The preacher will have to rise above any fear of facing this new generation.

of wonderful technology. Computers, tablets, podcasts, Facebook, Twitter, live streaming, e-mail, e-giving, iPhones, iBooks, iPads, Droids, and other electronic aids are found everywhere. The preacher must not fight using these and other tools. Rather, he or she must affirm them and use them to his or her advantage. More on the use of these tools will be discussed in a later chapter.

David was aware that Saul's equipment was not right for him or for the situation he faced. He refused to enter an unfamiliar situation with unfamiliar weapons. When the preacher faces a new challenge, he must be flexible and faithful in perfecting what works for the time and place of ministry.

The faithful have always faced new challenges and risen to the task.

- Moses faced the Red Sea, the deserts, and wilderness, but he rose to the challenge.
- Daniel and his friends faced a fiery furnace and a lion's den, but put their trust in God.
- Elijah faced a drought and an angry king. He was outnumbered and even had to deal with depression, but he met the challenge.
- Others have faced enemies and foes, but rose to the challenge. What about those who faced the challenges of segregation, racism, prejudice, but met those challenges head on?
- What about those who have faced hard times and have not known what to do, but were able to conquer their fears and their foes?

David understood that what may have worked for Saul would not work for him. He used what he had perfected. He went down to a nearby brook and picked up five smooth stones. He needed something that had been touched by living water. He chose stones because they were solid and had been tried and tested over time. He chose five of them because he needed the grace of God.

He chose five smooth stones and a slingshot because the slingshot reminded him that with God, he had the right stuff to take on Goliath.

The preacher must discern what works and what needs to be improved upon. Things that work in one setting may not work in another. The challenge of this book is to encourage the preacher to be honest and truthful and to identify the things that are no longer effective in reaching a new generation.

Questions for Discussion and Reflection:
1. What unfamiliar places have you found yourself in as a preaching?
2. Describe your emotion when in that unfamiliar place.
3. What role did faith play during your time of uncertainty?
4. What things have you tried in preaching that do not fit you?
5. What new things are you willing to try for the purpose of enhancing your preaching?

CHAPTER FIVE

PREACHING IN A SHIFTING CULTURE CONTEXT

The priest of Zeus, whose temple was just outside the city, brought oxen and garlands to the gates; he and the crowds wanted to offer sacrifice. When the apostles Barnabas and Paul heard of it, they tore their clothes and rushed out into the crowd, shouting, "Friends, why are you doing this? We are mortals just like you, and we bring you good news, that you should turn from these worthless things to the living God, who made the heaven and the earth and the sea and all that is in them."

—Acts 14:13–15 NRSV

It's a Different World

Chapter 14 of the book of Acts records a segment of the first missionary journey of Paul and his trusted companion, Barnabas. They formed their close relationship in Antioch. Barnabas, who was known as a great encourager, was sent to Antioch by the church to minister to those in Antioch who believed. When Barnabas arrived in Antioch and assessed the situation, he determined that he needed other spiritual gifts to assist him. He sent for Paul, who joined him and assisted with the new church. As a result of their work, believers were first called Christians in Antioch.

As Paul and Barnabas worked together in Antioch and Iconium, their fruitful ministry started to become a problem, and their lives were threatened. Seeking to escape from danger, they left Iconium and traveled by way of Lycaonia to the cities of Lystra and Derbe. Upon arriving in Lystra, Paul began to do what he did best which was to preach the gospel.

It seems it did not matter where Paul found himself. There was always one thing on his agenda and that was to preach Christ and his crucifixion. Preaching was a part of him. It was in his bones. It was what he had been commissioned to do and what he was called and compelled to do. The amazing thing about Paul was that he was always comfortable with any culture and in any context. He always had a word that was in season, and he was more than ready to share it. Strangely, he did not require a huge crowd or a packed house, nor did he require all of the trappings that many need today. He had no need for an elaborately decorated sanctuary. He did not require a praise and worship team to set the atmosphere nor a Hammond organ or electronic keyboard to provide melodious music or to back him up when he ended his sermon. He didn't need a guaranteed honorarium. He just came preaching. It could have been in a safe and secure synagogue, on a street corner, or in a small storefront. He only needed an audience of two or three. It was all the same to him when it came to declaring the gospel. For Paul, preaching was no mere performance. It contained the power of God that could transform a person's life and change the human condition. In his writings, "Preaching to the Postmodern Generation," Peyton Jones says,

> Preaching goes straight to the mind and heart. It is not philosophical in nature, although it has the potential for turning somebody's thinking upside down. Preaching can rip worldview inside out. Only a few things actually penetrate down to the depths of our soul, a childhood memory; a one of a kind life time experience, the birth of a child. In a world where so few things actually move us to the core of our being, preaching stands out as the greatest potential force for dislodging humanity's wheels out of its dark jungle.[25]

With a clear understanding of the power of preaching, and what it meant to his life and what it could mean to others, Paul seized every opportunity to declare the gospel of the kingdom of God.

Paul was in Lystra by default. It was not a planned trip, nor had an invitation been extended to him, as had happened when he saw a night vision and heard a voice saying, "Come over to Macedonia and help us." Rather, the situation in Iconium had forced him to flee, and he ended up in Lystra.

Like Paul, preachers today may find themselves in places by default. There are areas of life and ministry that are not chosen by

---

[25] Peyton Jones, "Preaching to the Postmodern Generation," accessed April 7, 2015, http://www.gospel-preaching.com/resources/Preaching%20To%20The%20Postmodern%20Generation.pdf.

us but chosen for us. Circumstances will often carry us to places we would not select.

Rather than complain about where they were and why they were there, Paul and Barnabas embraced the philosophy that "all things work together for good to those who love God and who are called according to his purpose."[26] What may have worked for evil, God could bring something good out of it. Paul decided to take advantage of the opportunity, and he proceeded to preach the word of God in Lystra.

Lystra was a Greek-speaking Roman colony ruled by the Roman government. There may have been only a few Jews living in Lystra at the time, such as Timothy; his mother, Eunice; and his grandmother Lois. Upon arriving in Lystra, Paul found himself in the heart of Greek culture. This would have been a challenge for Paul because he was a Jew and a strict one at that.

He came from the tribe of Benjamin, he had been circumcised on the eighth day, and he was a Hebrew of Hebrews. As it related to his religious training, he was a Pharisee, had the equivalent of an Ivy League education, and was trained by the scholar Gamaliel. Paul the Jew, with his straight collar, found himself in Greek-speaking Lystra- the "hood" so to speak. This was the kind of place where people did not read Bibles and hadn't heard about the God of Abraham and Sarah, Isaac and Rebekah. Folk in Lystra couldn't care less about attending church, paying tithes, or even listening to gospel music. However, Paul did not allow the culture to set his agenda. Rather, he set the agenda for the culture. Since there were no synagogues in Lystra, he found a crowd in the marketplace, grabbed a box, made it into a pulpit, and started preaching. As he preached, a certain man sat nearby. He had been crippled from birth, and it was said he never walked.

The fact that he never walked suggests that he had never stepped foot in anybody's church, sanctuary, or synagogue. He may have been

---

[26] Rom. 8:28 (KJV)

dropped off at the marketplace by friends or a family member so he could beg for money. In such proximity to Paul, he heard Paul's message.

Know Your Audience

I am convinced that if we preach, someone will hear. If we preach, some sinner will be saved. If we preach, someone will be touched. According to Mark Gomez, there are four levels of audiences one needs to know when preaching. The first level is those that the sermon was intended to reach. The second level is those who are indirectly listening to you, i.e. the unintended audience that happens to be sitting close enough to overhear your conversation, though you are not thinking of them while you are speaking. The third level is the unintended audience that is affected indirectly by your words. You did not say anything directly to them, but they heard your message later-maybe by way of a recording or through others who passed the message on. The fourth level is those who, in the past, we would not have needed to consider as much as we do now. This last audience is looking for mistakes in our words so that they can use them against us.

In the Lystra marketplace, the crippled man would have been in the second level. Paul was not preaching directly to him, but indirectly he heard the message. Something must have happened so that Paul saw him and he saw Paul. It may have been similar to what happened with Peter and John in Acts chapter 3 where they encountered a lame man. When Peter saw him, "he fastened his eyes on him." I am not sure if Paul's eyes were fastened on this lame man or if the lame man's eyes were fastened on Paul. At any rate, they made eye contact.

This was no mere accident or coincidence. It appears that a divine setup had taken place. Paul could see in the man's eye a desire for something; perhaps a desire to walk for the first time. It appears that

Paul's preaching planted a seed of faith in the man's life, and now something was budding.

The lame man's presence in the marketplace is a clear reminder that there is a world out there that's waiting to hear the gospel that we preach. Some may not be aware of their need. Nonetheless, the need exists. Countless individuals need to be touched by the love of God and need to hear of the grace of God.

Though the lame man had come from the streets of Lystra, Paul was not afraid him. He did not shy away from him, nor did he ignore the man's condition. He did not walk by him as if he had a contagious disease. Even though the crippled man was different—he looked different, he talked different, he dressed different, his life was moving to a different kind of beat—when Paul saw him, he paused to minister to the man's need. Paul preached, and there was such power in his preaching, the man was arrested by his words.

At the conclusion of his sermon, Paul shouted to the man, "stand up on your feet and walk." At the command, the man who had never stood on his feet, stood up by the power of God.

This moment shook the community. People in Lystra had never seen anything like this before. Word got around town about the man who had been lame but was no longer so because a stranger had commanded him to stand up. People ran from everywhere to see this wonder. They came out of their houses, closed down their fruit stands, left their animals in the pastures, and ran to see the man who was trying out his new legs. Upon seeing the lame man's miracle, the people stood in awe of Paul and Barnabas.

Experiencing a Cultural Shift

This is where a complication in the text occurs. The people of Lystra wanted to honor Paul and Barnabas. That was not a problem in itself. The manner in which they wanted to honor them, though, created a huge problem. They sought to deify Paul and Barnabas, declaring "the gods have come down to us in human form!" The people even decided *which* gods had come to visit them. They started with Paul. Since he was doing most of the speaking, he must be Hermes, the Greek god of oratory and the inventor of speech. They called Barnabas Zeus, perhaps because of his size, as Zeus was the head of the Greek pantheon.

Paul and Barnabas found themselves right smack in the midst of a pluralistic setting. Some were saying the gods had come to earth; others were saying God had worked through humans; and still others wanted to run them out of town, saying they were imposters.

The manner in which the people of Lystra interpreted this healing experience reflected their polytheistic beliefs. Their culture was quite different from Paul's. Paul worshipped the one true and living God, and they worshiped many gods. Their values and realities were vastly different. The ways in which they each understood and interpreted life was based upon the culture that had shaped their minds and their belief systems.

> The people of Lystra held to an old legend that at one time Zeus and Hermes had visited the city in disguise. An elderly couple had entertained them, not realizing that they were two gods. As a result of their being snubbed, Zeus and Hermes severely punished the rest of the people, leaving the old couple as guardians of the temple. The people of Lystra wanted to be certain that they did not make this mistake again. They hailed Barnabas as Zeus and Paul as Hermes. [27]

[27] *Acts: Unlocking the Scriptures for You*, [Computer File], electronic ed., Libronix Digital Library System (Cincinnati, OH: Standard, 1987), Acts 14:8 ff.

This is a digital-clear picture of the times in which we live and the culture in which we preach. Preachers in the twenty-first century are called to address people who think differently, act differently, and see things through a different lens. That lens which is shaped by television, the Internet,

> Preachers in the twenty-first century are called to address people who think differently, act differently, and see things through a different lens.

and music, and is often foreign to the preacher's ears. The world has gone through a value shift. Some may live right next door or in your backyard, yet their experiences are so different. Some can be right around the corner from a church, but have yet to be touched by the church.

Not so many years ago, it was common for people to have some measure of religious background and biblical literacy. However, there's been a drastic shift. Religious training and biblical language have all but vanished from the minds of a new generation. Humanistic philosophies and antisupernatural presuppositions dominate in most segments of our population.

Preaching in a Context of Conflicting Values

A preacher may value one thing, and his or her values may be rejected by those he or she is trying to reach with the gospel. The previous generation may have believed that music should be positive, meaningful, and uplifting, but there is a segment of our culture that makes a noise that seems to be empty and meaningless. Some degrade and demean women, our mothers, and our daughters.

A preacher may believe in oral communication and hold to the idea that people ought to touch each other with the love of God. They should talk things through and work things out, speak to each other in the morning and throughout the day, but we live in a culture that makes optimal use of technology. Many would rather text than talk, and air out differences on Facebook rather than face-to-face. The things that my generation would argue over with words now cause the younger generation pulls out guns and takes the lives of their opponents without a second thought.

The preacher may hold in high esteem a weekly visit to the sanctuary, where the songs of Zion are sung by a choir, the sacred text is read, and the congregation engages in prayer and listens to the sermon. But now, there is a culture that is not interested in gathering in the sanctuary, let alone sitting and listening to a thirty-minute sermon. The preacher may dress up, put on a nice shirt, tie, and jacket, but there is a group who only wear jeans—and wear them only halfway up to their waist. The girls' skirts are short and their dresses are low cut.

Although Paul and Barnabas found themselves in a different cultural context, that was not the only problem or the biggest problem. Paul may have been able to handle that shift in context. After all, he was the one who said, "I became all things to all men that I might win some."[28] The larger problem was that the people of Lystra sought to impose their cultural beliefs and practices on Paul and Barnabas.

The people referred to them as gods. The priest of Jupiter, whose temple was on the outskirts of the city, showed up with oxen dressed with garlands for a sacrifice unto Paul and Barnabas. The culture wanted to suck them in and to superimpose itself on them. Paul and Barnabas had to resist the temptation of getting pulled into the culture, by refusing to accept the sacrifice and denying the people a party of a lifetime. Remember: it was Paul who wrote "And be not conformed to this world: but be ye transformed by the renewing of your mind, that ye may prove what is that good, and acceptable, and

---

[28] 1 Cor. 9:23 (KJV)

perfect, will of God." Romans 12:2 (KJV). He now had to take a dose of his own medicine.

I wonder how hard it was for Paul and Barnabas to resist the temptation to be glorified and deified by these people. Preachers know all too well the temptation to inhale praise. There is something about human nature that has an appetite for loftiness. Who more than preachers enjoy receiving accolades and getting a pat on the back? Preachers know the need to remain true to their calling, yet the success of a ministry can cause one to feel deserving of material trappings. Who wouldn't like to be the pastor of a megachurch, live in a mansion, drive a luxury vehicle, and be surrounded by security and armor bearers? Who wouldn't like to say that that they preach to a packed house every Sunday? Who wouldn't like to be invited to stand behind the major pulpits across the country and be in high demand?

Paul and Barnabas had to resist the temptation of falling into the snare of a culture that would define them, when it was their role to transform that culture.

Thus the relevant question is: What makes for effective preaching in a shifting culture? I think that the story of Paul and Barnabas in Lystra offers a couple of clues and presents a powerful demonstration of how a preacher can shift preaching for a shifting culture.

Effective Preaching in a Shifting Culture

First, effective preaching begins with a spirit of humility. Paul and Barnabas tore their clothes, ran among the people, and said, "We are men of like passion, as you." The tearing away of their clothes was a sign of humility. They went before the people humbled rather than exalted. They connected with them at the core of their beings. Though the crowd regarded them highly, as a result of Paul's anointing and ability to work miracles, Paul did not approach them from a lofty position. He was not the Reverend Dr., nor the bishop, nor the apostle. Rather, he met them as a man with like passions. Paul knew that the people needed to see and know that first and foremost, he was just a human being like them.

So he disrobed himself. He removed his clergy collar and took off his long embroidered robe with the doctoral bars on the sleeves and the embroidered cross on the velvet panel along the front. He removed his dazzling diamond cross from around his neck and took off his oversized fourteen-carat gold ring. He released his quarter-size cufflinks from his French cuffs and took off his white silk shirt. Had he been a female, he would have also taken his hair down and removed his nail polish. Divested in this way, he went to be among the crowd.

He was not interested in demonstrating the theological skills he had gained as a student, nor of boasting how long he'd been around the church as a layperson or as a leader.

See, what Paul understood was that he had something in common with the people and they had something in common with him. They might not share the same views and values, but as mere mortals, they all needed the grace of God. All people have sinned and come short of the glory of God. At the core, it really does not matter who we are, where we've been, and what we believe. First and foremost, we are just men and women with a common bond. That's really the connection. Paul remembered that where he was now was not where he'd always been. Though reared in a believing home, he had not always believed. He once had a different perspective on things, but one day he met Jesus for himself. But for the grace of God, Paul would have been in the same place he had been in before.

We have all made some decisions of which we are not proud. We, too, have bought into the fashion and styles of our times. Come on and tell the truth. You know something about the vices of life. We have not always been in church or in Christ. Some of us used to get high, suffer from hangovers, and have done things that we do not care to discuss.

People are people. It does not matter who we are or where we come from, for we are all plagued by the same human predicament.

Sometimes others need to hear that we know something about what they're going through.

We know about the struggles of being single, about losing our jobs, about struggling to make ends meet. We know what it's like to try to come up with the money to pay for tuition, buy books, and put gas in our cars so we can get to class. We know what it's like to go through a divorce and to have challenges in our relationships. We know the struggles of rearing children. We are preachers, but our children have not always been angels. We know what you feel, we know how you think, but we also found out that there is a more excellent way.

That is what we declare: that our Lord came among us so that he could save us. He met us at the point of our humanity. He did not remain in the lofty levels of heaven. He did not save us from a distance. He did not send someone else to take his place.

Rather, he came among us. He

- was fully God and fully human
- entered the birth canal of a young woman
- rolled around in amniotic fluid for nine months
- humbled himself

His parents did not have health care that would get them a room in a maternity ward in Bethlehem, so he had to be born in a public clinic called a stable.

His parents did not have Internet access so that news of his birth could be announced and go viral around the world. He had to make the announcement by word of mouth, by way of a group of shepherds who were watching their flock by night. Jesus grew up in a hood in a place called Nazareth. He was humble; and when he did decide to be elevated as King of Kings and Lord of Lords, he did not come into town riding on a white stallion, but on a lowly donkey. He humbled himself and became obedient unto death, even the death of the cross.

If you and I are going to be effective in reaching a shifting culture, we have to practice some humility. But that's not all. The text indicates that Paul demonstrated—or should I say, practiced—good homiletics.

After Paul tore his clothes and ran into the crowd, the next thing that he did was to preach. However, what you will notice in the text is that there was a shift in his preaching. When he had first arrived in Lystra, he'd had his sermon well prepared. It was homiletically structured, exegetically sound, with illustrations in the right place, and polished for the crowd, but it was the wrong sermon. The crowd heard the sermon but was unchanged by it. This was a different crowd from what Paul was accustomed. His preaching did not change them, for they continued to believe in polytheism. Paul knew that if he was to be effective in his preaching, he would have to be flexible and adaptable to various settings. His message and delivery had to fit the audience he was addressing. Because he was seminary trained and a faithful student of homiletics, he was flexible and skillful in effective preaching, preaching that hit the bull's eye.

So let me ask: Have you revisited your preaching lately? Have you examined its effectiveness on the audience that you are preaching to Sunday after Sunday? Or are you still preaching the same old thing, the same old way to a brand-new generation?

Notice that Paul did not abandon preaching itself, for preaching was still the order of the day. These people were not literate in the Old Testament, so he could not speak about the history of the Jews and what God had done to Abraham and the people of Israel, as he had in the synagogue of Antioch. These people knew nothing about the patriarchs and kings of Israel.

In fact, they were in a Greek-speaking colony, and reverted to their native language and started speaking in the tongue of the Lycaonians. Paul understood that just because a person is talking, that does not mean there is communication. Someone once said that the biggest problem in communication is the illusion that it has taken place. So Paul shifted the style and content of his preaching. We have a wonderful model of connecting and communicating with the audience in Jesus.

Jesus specialized in custom-made preaching. He carefully and sensitively crafted his message to accommodate the nature and the life situations of the people he was talking to. He began his communication where people were and not where he thought they ought to be. He recognized and respected such factors as their world view, culture, previous knowledge and experiences, and attention span. He respected each person as a unique individual. He talked the people's language and used common terms (the kingdom of heaven), common issues (the Messiah), and common images (bread, water). That's the kind of preacher Paul was, and it's the kind of preacher, student, and church person that is needed in our world today.

Paul and Barnabas did not stop with the demonstration of humility and good homiletics, though. Paul demonstrated that the content of preaching must reach the heart of the people. That was what he did. He went for the heart. He told the crowd to turn from useless, empty, and vain living that did not bring satisfaction or fulfillment, and to turn to the living God that had made heaven and earth; the God who gave us rain from heaven and fruitful seasons, filling our hearts with food and gladness. When Paul started to talk about rain, fruitful seasons, and food, he got the crowd's attention because these things were important to the people. The content of Paul's message met them where they were. They knew something about the god of rain and the god of agriculture.

It has been said that to effectively communicate to people, we need to "scratch 'em where they itch." That is, we need to reach people at their point of need in a language they understand. People today are continually bombarded with messages via radio, TV, billboards, newspapers, e-mails, Facebook, texts, and so on. However, the only messages they attend to are those that speak directly to their perceived needs and interests. They filter out everything else. Meeting people at their point of need is the most powerful and effective means of communication. In fact, it is the key to opening closed minds. Once again, Jesus is our perfect model for preaching.

When Jesus preached or taught, he always addressed people at their point of need. For example, he asked the man who had been around the pool of Bethesda: "Do you want to be made well?" When he saw Zacchaeus up in a sycamore tree, he said to him, "Come down out of your tree. I'm going to your house today." When he heard blind Bartimaeus call his name, he stopped and asked what Bartimaeus wanted him to do for him.

Jesus preached about eternal life, about absolute truth, about human wholeness and about spiritual freedom. He told stories such as about "The Good Samaritan" and "The Prodigal Son." He asked questions, such as, "What good will it be for a man if he gains the whole world, yet forfeits his soul?"[29] or "Who of you by worrying can add a single hour to his life?"[30] He used visual aids, such as lilies, sheep and shepherds, and wine bottles.

Paul demonstrated humility, good homiletics, and he got to the heart of the matter, but those things alone do not make a great sermon. A great sermon, well structured, exegetically sound, with crystal-clear illustration and a strong close, is most effective when it is accompanied by the power of God.

When Paul first preached in Lystra, the power of God was demonstrated through the healing of a lame man. But then the power of God was demonstrated through the preacher himself.

No sooner had Paul closed his sermon and stepped out of the pulpit, than the crowd he had escaped from in Antioch arrived and stirred up the people in Lystra. Paul and Barnabas had fled to Lystra to avoid being stoned in Antioch and Iconium. But now, those Jews

[29] Matt. 16:26a (KJV)
[30] Luke 12:25 (KJV)

had caught up with them and, according to the text, they persuaded the people of Lystra to stone Paul.

So they dragged Paul out of the city, stoned him, and left him for dead.

But while Paul's body lay limp and helpless on the ground, the disciples gathered around him. The text does not say what they did. The only thing I can surmise is that when saints get together and hold hands, somebody must be praying. What we do know is that Paul got up. What a demonstration of power!

Now, his getting up was a miracle in itself, but that was not the end of the story. Paul did not resign from preaching. He did not decide to leave the church. He did not run away from the crowd this time. Rather, he went right back to the city and started preaching.

Why would a preacher who had been dragged out of the city and stoned for preaching go back to the city and preach again?

- Why are some still preaching today after all that they have been through?
- Why are some still in seminary, given the challenges they are going through right now?
- Why are some still in churches with as much as they have had to endure?

Like Paul, the necessity is laid upon those who are called to carry the gospel. "Woe to me if I do not preach the gospel!"[31]

The preacher may have been called to preach to those with whom he or she is familiar, but he is also called to those who may be completely different and who are hearing the gospel for the first time. In the next chapter, we will see Jesus as a perfect example of how to preach to those who may not be a part of the regular church crowd.

---

[31] 1 Cor. 9:16 (KJV)

Questions for Discussion and Reflection:

1. What cultural shifts have you recognized lately?
2. Have these shifts affected your preaching in any way?
3. How comfortable are you in preaching to those who do not fit into your context?
4. Do you feel the pressure to fit into this new culture in order to survive?
5. How can you adjust your message or method to make it effective in this day and age?

CHAPTER SIX

SHAPING YOUR PREACHING FOR AN UNCHURCHED CROWD

> But he had to go through Samaria.
>
> —John 4:4 NRSV

One of the great joys of ministry is baptizing those who express faith for the first time. During my thirty-year tenure as pastor of Gethsemane Baptist Church, there have been only a few months when the baptismal pool has not been filled with water. I have watched countless individuals walk down the aisle of the church and give their lives to the Lord Jesus Christ, and then follow up by submitting to water baptism. I have also noticed that there are some months when more persons than usual make commitments to the faith. During the various seasons in the cycle of a church's life, the harvests of souls have been greater in some than in others. Nonetheless, a steady flow of people keep the baptismal pool filled with fresh water. The age range of those who have been baptized expands from the very young to the very old. The blessing of having tenure as a pastor in one place is that you get to baptize the children of those you baptized earlier. Many of the people I baptized over the years grew up in Christian homes, and it was expected that at some point they would come to faith. On the other hand, there are those who heard the gospel message for the first time; and upon hearing it, they believed and acted on what they heard.

Baptisms serve as an indicator that God is still at work in the world redeeming the lost. It is a reminder that the world needs the saving grace of God, and that God has not abandoned his mission to reclaim the world or his method of redemption. Such an affirmation is also a reminder for the preacher that preaching must take into consideration those who may be hearing the gospel for the first time. The sermon cannot be one dimensional or directed exclusively to the regular attendees of church.

> A preacher who is able to proclaim the gospel only to believers who are already deeply Christianized in vocabulary and concept will not be able to proclaim the gospel to people who are not only ignorant of basic biblical content and terminology, but who have already

adopted stances toward spirituality and religion that
are deeply at odds with what the Bible says. We are
required to help them erase certain files and parts of
files that clash irremediably with the truth of Scripture
that we are trying to write onto their minds. These
are challenges that exerted a few pressures on most
Christian preachers in the Western world a bare half-
century ago.[32]

If the twenty-first century preacher takes these words to heart,
then he or she must seek to be multidimensional in the pulpit.
The sermon must be shaped and sensitive to the churched and the
unchurched, the saved and the seeker.

Make it Relevant

As the future unfolds, the numbers of those who have little or no
familiarity with the Christian faith, and who will give listen to preaching
whether in the church sanctuary or in some other setting, is sure to rise.
This may mean that preachers will find themselves preaching to a larger
population of those who have never been to church or have little or no
knowledge of the faith. Therefore, preaching will have to strive for a
greater level of relevance. In his new book *What They Didn't Teach You in
Seminary,* James Emery White stresses the importance of relevance in
effective communication. He says,

> Being relevant has nothing to do with watering
> down the truth of the gospel. It has nothing to
> do with removing all references to sin, the cross
> or commitment. It does not mean having to stay

---

[32] Leland Ryken and Todd A. Wilson, eds., *Preach the Word: Essays on
Expository Preaching in Honor of R. Kent Hughes,* (Wheaton, IL: Crossway
Books, 2007), 184.

> with topical messages that deal solely with issues
> such as parenting, family, marriage, self-image and
> relationships. All I'm suggesting is to avoid giving
> a 19th or 20th-century message to a 21st century
> audience.[33]

In my estimation, one of the greatest preachers who ever lived and was relevant in any setting was Jesus. One of the greatest times when he exemplified his sense of relevance is in the story of the woman at the well, as recorded in the fourth book of the Gospel of Saint John.

The pericope opens with Jesus needing to go through Samaria. The general understanding is that at that time, Jews would avoid going through Samaria. Their avoidance was so strong, they would go out of their way to avoid coming in contact with the Samaritans. However, in places that others deemed off limits, Jesus saw great opportunities for expanding the kingdom of God. By going through Samaria, he demonstrated that the preacher must be willing to take the gospel beyond the boundaries that have been set by others. The future of preaching must take into consideration the need to carry the gospel message to where people are, whether physically or in terms of a sermon's content. Jesus saw Samaria as fertile ground and took on the task of taking his ministry to an unreached population.

So, imagine that it was right at noontime in Samaria. The sun was at its peak and the temperature was sweltering hot. Most folks were racing toward cool places of comfort, such as air-conditioned rooms. The factory whistles were blowing, and those who had been working all morning were putting their tools down, securing their merchandise, and heading to the break room. Housewives had put

---

[33] "Preaching, Leading the Church, Proclaiming the Word," *Relevant Preaching*, July 25, 2011, accessed April 8, 2015, http://www.preaching.com/resources/articles/11653970/

their children down for a nap, turned on their televisions, and sat down to watch Sherri Shepherd or Steve Harvey or Family Feud. Still others were enjoying conversations with each other, as this was the time of day to retreat from the toil of the morning.

While much of the city had come to a brief standstill, one woman was just getting ready to start her day. She appeared with her face hidden by a scarf wrapped around her upper body. The scarf would prevent the wind from blowing sand in her eyes, but it also shielded her identity. She really did not choose this time to go out. Rather, the time chose her. This was the time of day when she could avoid the crowds. Avoid hearing the mean and unkind things people would say about her. Avoid the sight of people whispering about her mistakes in life.

With a water pot on top of her head, her eyes focused straight ahead, and her heart racing, she hoped she would not run into anyone she knew while she went to the well to retrieve her daily supply of water.

She lived in isolation and shame. Her own family had disassociated from her. The community looked down on her- not to mention that she was a female in a male-dominated society. Things had not gone all that well for her. For one reason or another, she had not made the best choices in life. She tried, but time and time again, things had not worked in her favor. By now, she was dealing with low or no self-esteem. She blamed herself for the things that had not gone right in her life. She was bitter, broken, and belittled.

She really believed it was over for her. Maybe that was what other people said to her, and it was what she felt about herself. She was without dreams, visions, or plans for the future. She did not look for anything or expect anything different. She simply existed and did what she needed to do in order to survive. Family members and friends no longer cared enough to speak encouraging words to her. She had no support system. This was the best that life had to offer her: a trip in the heat of the day to a well that left her thirsty.

This was the condition of the woman Jesus met off the beaten path. He did not wait for her to come to him; he went to where she was. He did not meet her on the steps of the temple but in the depth of her own struggles. The condition of this woman may resemble the condition of many in the world today, a condition of hopelessness, aimlessness, and shame. The sermon must attempt to reach those people, and it must do so with compassion, understanding, and love.

Like the woman in this story, the preacher and those who have been in and around the church for some time have not always made good choices. The choices may not have been as devastating as this woman's, but many live with regrets, with broken dreams, broken promises, and broken relationships.

We all have people who have pushed us to the side and refuse to have anything to do with us. We have a spouse who decided they wanted nothing to do with us. We have parents we do not get along with, siblings who do not speak to us, and friends who have stabbed us in the back.

We too have tried one thing or another and experienced failure and defeat. We started out and kept the pace, but then we did not finish. We know what it is like to go home and feel as though we are all alone. We know what it is like to be trapped in our own skin and unable to break free. We know what it feels like to have things in our pasts for which we are ashamed, and we have people whom we'd rather avoid and not have to look in the face. The same gospel that met us where we were is the same gospel that will meet others where they are.

Keep it Real

Jesus made an adjustment to his sermon for the purpose of entering into the woman's world so that he could usher her into his world. His strategy was to address the immediate concerns of her life, so he asked her for a drink of water. He did not ask her because he was thirsty. Rather, he asked her because he was acutely aware of her thirst. There are times when the Lord will ask for what he knows a person needs, fully aware that the person lacks what the Lord is asking for. When he asks for what a person does not have, he does so not because he is trying to get something from them, but he does so because is trying to give something to them.

He asked the woman for a drink of water because she was thirsty. She was thirsty for conversation. She was thirsty for companionship. And she was thirsty for communion with God.

That was the grace of God. If Jesus had not asked her for what she was thirsty for, she might not have ever acknowledged that she needed it. When he asked her for water, she revealed that she did not know where to get the water. She looked at Jesus and said, "The well is deep and you have nothing to draw with."

This was her first time meeting Jesus. She had not even heard about him, so she did not know what he could do for her. Jesus told her that he was the one who was able to meet her unmet needs. He shared with her that to continue drawing from the same old well would deliver the same old results. It was time for her to try something different and better.

The woman was sick and tired of the same old thing yielding her the same old results, and so she was willing to try something different. However, in order for the woman to experience the better way that Jesus knew, he had to communicate to her that there was a higher level of thinking. She just wanted water so that she could satisfy her physical thirst. She was like some people who come to the Lord because they are looking for something to quench their physical thirst.

Some come for the blessing. Some come because they want their bills paid. Some come because they want to find a Boo. Some come because they want a bigger house. Some come because they want a better and faster automobile. All that is fine, but if that is all you get, then you have nothing more than what you had at first, and you will be thirsty again.

Sometimes in order to get something better, you have to deal with the worst.

After asking the woman for water, Jesus said to her, "Go get your husband." She said that she had no husband." He said, "I know, you have had five and the one you have now is not your own." He was not condemning the woman. He was telling her to acknowledge that she needed more than what she had previously experienced. She could not get what the Lord had for her until she was willing to let go of what she had had in the past.

When Jesus started to relate to her on this level, she understood that he was talking about more than the physical, but that he was talking on the spiritual plane. She said, "Sir, I perceive that you are a prophet."

When to Talk Religion

More than experiencing a physical thirst, she was experiencing a spiritual thirst. It was then that Jesus revealed to her that he was the one for whom she had been looking. What others could not do for her, he could. Where others failed, he would not fail. Where others came up short, he made up the difference. What others could not fulfill and satisfy, he fulfilled and fully satisfied. Others felt she was undeserving, but he knew she was deserving.

He knew there was one thing the woman deserved, and that was the love of God. She may have been hated by the community and she may have even hated herself, but she was loved by God. She may have done wrong; and while God did not approve of her sin, he never removed his love for her. He loved her so much, he was willing to come to where she was. He did not wait until she got right. He came to her while she was in her mess.

The message that the preacher must proclaim to the world is simply the message that Jesus offered this woman: there is a God in Jesus who meets us in our past and brings us into a better future. He goes out of his way just for us. Regardless of what other people think about us or what other people say about us, he knows that we deserve his love. He knows that we deserve another chance and that we deserve better than what we have experienced in the past.

We deserve the future he has planned for us. We do not deserve it on the basis of our merit; we deserve it on the basis of his grace and mercy. He knows the thirst of the world, he knows the desires of people's hearts, he knows the longing of the soul, and he is the one that the preacher proclaims as all sufficient.

Jesus did not speak in spiritual terms or use religious jargon. He spoke to the relevant need of the woman. By no means was this a watering down of the gospel. Rather, he was seeking to build a bridge whereby he could get the woman's attention. The preacher may be able to use sermon topics and develop series that are relevant. By relevant I mean, addressing the real issues and situations that people deal with in their daily lives. The sermon must be effective as opposed to just sounding good. It must help the listener identify the folly of his or her current situation and bring to bear the good news of the gospel. The gospel must be presented as a tried, tested, and proven solution to the problems of the world.

The subject of the sermon is the hook that captures the audience's attention and compels the congregation to listen to the sermon. It is the door through which the preacher is able to enter the house and walk around every room of the listener's life. That is what Jesus did when he asked the woman to go and get her husband. He knew that the door was open and he had permission to enter the other rooms of the woman's life.

The role of the preacher is not to disseminate information, but to lead people to find the biblical meaning of a text in their lives.

Jesus said to her, "For thou hast had five husbands; and he whom thou now hast is not thy husband: in that saidist thou truly. The woman saith unto him, "Sir, I perceive that thou art a prophet. Our fathers worshiped in this mountain; and ye say, that in Jerusalem is the place where men ought to worship" (John 4:18–20 KJV). This is not to say that religious terms and conversation must be initiated by the listener, for the listener may not initiate such a conversation. However, it does suggest that the preacher should at least get off the front porch and go in through the front door of the listener's life before he or she sits down to have that spiritual conversation. That is to say, somewhere in the body of the sermon, not too early, the preacher will find a place to introduce and proclaim the gospel message.

Reaching Beyond the Sermon

Once the preacher comes to the place of proclaiming the gospel, he or she may consider sharing the message in such a way that it provides the audience an experience with the text. The role of the preacher is not to disseminate information, but to lead people to find the biblical meaning of a text in their lives. Remember: the world in which we live is full of colorful and creative images designed to draw people into a real world. Observe how media uses images these days rather than a convincing argument. It is what Frank Thomas calls "experiential preaching."

The Bible comes alive by means of an eyewitness style of picture painting and narration. The preacher stirs the five senses, and, as a result, the hearer does not just hear about John the Baptist in the past biblical times, rather John the Baptist is presented in the room, seen, heard, touched, and felt by all. James Forbes tells the story that Gardner Taylor was preaching the biblical story of the Prodigal Son. There was a moment when he said, "it looked like the boy was coming down the aisle.[34]

A shift occurring in preaching for the future might suggest a move from appealing to the cognitive to the emotive by offering the listener an experience.

A shift occurring in preaching for the future might suggest a move from appealing to the cognitive to the emotive by offering the listener an experience. It is said that people aren't necessarily changed by information; rather, they are changed by experience. One psychologist says "people are made of heart and brain, they think and they feel, and what they think and feel is real." There is a lot of information available nowadays, and people know a lot of things. However, knowing does not always translate to change. Change often occurs through experience. Think about your own life. Think of all of the things you know and ask yourself how what you know affects the things that you do. On the other hand, think of the experiences you've had and how those experiences have shaped the person that you are.

---

[34] Frank Thomas, *They Like to Never Quit Praising God: The Role of Celebration in Preaching* (Cleveland: The Pilgrim Press, 2013), Kindle edition, loc 186.

The sermon should seek to offer people an experience. One of the ways a sermon can help the listener to have an experience is through the use of images. For an example: we see with more than our mind's eye, we also hear with more than the mind's ear, smell with more than the mind's nose, feel with more the mind's muscles, and taste with more than the mind's tongue.

The preacher must first experience the text. He or she must bring all five senses to the text by walking around in it, looking to determine what can be seen, listening for what you can hear, thinking of what you may feel, smell, and taste. In John 4, when Jesus referenced worship "neither in this mountain, nor yet at Jerusalem" (John 4:21 KJV), he was using an image with which the woman was familiar. He was helping her to experience what he was sharing in a way that was real and eye-catching.

Should the preacher decide to make use of illustrations, the illustrations should be easy for the listener to recognize. The best illustrations are not always those found in books that are dated, but they should be fresh, current, and speak to matters in which the audience is familiar. If the preacher is alert to his or her daily experiences and surroundings, he or she will find an abundance of material to use as sermon illustrations. Be sure never to waste any good or bad experience. It might be the perfect thing to include in a sermon that is yet to be preached. When the preacher makes use of fresh, real-life illustrations the audience can easily connect with, the sermon becomes real and believable. The sermon is no longer just something that the preacher is talking about. It is what the preacher has lived and experienced.

The preacher should also consider making use of a sermon structure when developing a sermon. We have all heard sermons that seem to go all over the place. Those who are new to church, worship, and preaching may already be having difficulty comprehending the church's rituals and the preacher's message. That difficulty increases when the sermon is hard to follow. Using a sermon structure makes it easier for the audience to grasp and understand the ideas and concepts the preacher is presenting. It also helps the preacher to organize his or her thoughts and keep the sermon focused. The use of a sermon structure increases the chances of the preacher accomplishing the sermon's goal. Even if a preacher is currently using a sermon structure, it is a good idea to add various structures to the toolbox to allow for flexibility and freshness. Many good sermon structures are available, and preachers should seek to discover the structure or structures that work best for them.

Finally, keep the sermons simple. A preacher may be tempted to demonstrate his or her intelligence. It is often self-gratifying to be impressive and loquacious. However, the preacher must always remember the purpose of the sermon. The sermon should seek to glorify the kingdom of God, not the preacher. The preacher should seek to hear Jesus saying, "well done, thou good and faithful servant," rather than the congregation declaring how awesome a sermon and its presentation were.

Remember: Jesus always preached in such a way that people could easily understand his message. Dr. James Merritt in an article entitled, "Pastoral Leadership in a Postmodern World" says,

> I have learned both by experience and by study of the Scripture that human beings tend to complicate the simple. When I read about Jesus, I find that He came to simplify the complicated. There is a reason why, for example, Jesus spent the vast majority of his ministry telling stories. Almost two-thirds of the gospel of Luke is a story—just one parable, one story, after another. If Jesus gave a seminar on preaching, I'm convinced one of the things He would tell us is "paint word pictures." Tell stories. Say the truth in

such a way that common, ordinary people, even little children, can understand it and get a handle on it.[35]

The prophet Habakkuk was told to "write the vision, and make it plain upon tables, so he may run that reads it" (Hab. 2:2b). In the blog, Atomic Reach, a post on August 8, 2014, entitled "7 Ways You Can Impact Your Message with Better Language" noted:

> The best storytellers, the ones that you remember, are able to deliver their message plainly, using real examples. I always go back to songs of our childhood. I know how a bus moves forward because the wheels on the bus go round and round. Sure there is way more to it, but frankly I don't care about the inner workings of a vehicle, just like your audience doesn't likely care what's under your sophisticated technology. You need to keep it simple and relatable. If your ten-year-old nephew can understand the pitch, so will your audience.[36]

My dear mother, who now sleeps with the Lord, was not an educated woman. I was blessed to have her alive when I first started preaching. She was one of my greatest supporters. She accompanied me to countless engagements. I always wanted to preach in such a manner that my mother could understand my message. Preacher, keep it simple, and the Holy Spirit will do the rest.

---

[35] James Merritt, "Pastoral Leadership in a Postmodern World," February 2003, accessed February 18, 2015, www.uu.edu/centers/rglee/fellows/fall03/merritt.htm.

[36] Ira Haberman, "7 Ways You Can Impact Your Message with Better Language," Atomic Reach, August 8, 2014, accessed February 18, 2015, https://www.atomicreach.com/blog/6-ways-you-can-impact-with-better-language/.

As a preacher seeks to reach a new crowd, it is important that his or her message stays rooted and grounded within the context of scripture. In the next chapter, we will discuss the importance of preaching the Word.

Discussion Questions and Reflection:

1. Are you comfortable preaching to an audience that has little or no experience with church?

2. How well are you able to adopt the language in your sermon to an unchurched crowd?

3. How well do you currently make use of the five senses and images in your preaching?

4. Would you say that your preaching appeals more to the intellect or to life experiences?

5. What sermon(s) structure/style do you use the most when developing your message?

6. Can a ten-year-old easily understand your sermon?

CHAPTER SEVEN

PREACHING WITH A HANDHELD DEVICE

The Lord said to him, "What is that in your hand?"

—Exodus 4:2 NRSV

Two powerful questions regarding the future of preaching are recorded in the first two verses of Exodus's chapter 4. One is raised by Moses, who responds to the call to serve as God's ambassador while the other is raised by God in response to some critical concerns of Moses. In my estimation, both questions are worthy of examination by the modern-day preacher. In this chapter, I will focus upon only one of them, God's question to Moses: "What is that in thine hand?"

Following an unsuccessful refusal to accept God's call upon his life, Moses finally surrendered and agreed to deliver God's message to Pharaoh. Earlier, God had appeared to Moses in the most unusual way. Moses was going about his daily chores, shepherding sheep on the far side of the Midian desert, when he heard a strange sound and smelled a strange odor. There before him was a bush on fire, but it was not consumed. He would learn that this was no common fire or ordinary bush. He was experiencing an eternal flame that would ignite his God-given purpose and extinguish his own personal pursuits.

From that strange and unusual sight emerged the voice of God, calling him by name in the most compelling way. This was a strange encounter that Moses—or anyone else, for that matter—could not ignore. As happened with Saul of Tarsus on the road to Damascus, the voice of God must be heard and cannot be disregarded. Moses knew that geographically he was in Midian, but he did not know that appositionally he was in the presence of the Eternal. To aid and assist in proper protocol, God instructed Moses to remove his shoes and informed him that he was standing on holy ground. Of course, God, who is a complete gentleman, introduced himself to Moses, and told Moses the reason for his appearance. He had heard the cry of his people in their oppression and had come to deliver them. He was inviting Moses to join him and help in their deliverance.

Like most who are called by God, Moses was startled and taken aback by the invitation. He hardly knew what to say. He could only express his feelings of inadequacy. Beating himself on the chest, he expressed his disbelief that the God of the universe would consider using someone like him for such an important assignment. He told the one who knew him from the inside out, who had created him in his image and had designed his life before he was born, that he was unqualified and ill-equipped, as he often stuttered when he spoke. Moses presented to God one scenario after another, seeking to prove his inadequacy, only to discover that God had a rebuttal for each of his objections. Having run out of excuses, he accepted the call and prepared for the assignment. But he had just one question left: "What if they do not believe me or listen to me?"

God responded by asking Moses a simple question: "What is that in thine hand?" "A staff," Moses replied. Moses was concerned about the authenticity of this message. He wanted to be certain that those who heard his message would believe him. However, God assured him that the authenticity and affirmation of his message would be delivered through the device in his hand, and demonstrated how this would be accomplished. He instructed Moses to throw his staff on the ground. When he did so, the staff became a snake, and he ran from it. God told him to pick up the snake, and it became a staff again. Knowing that Moses, like most, would need more proof, God commanded him to put his hands inside his garment. When Moses did so, the color of his skin was changed and became white as snow. God then instructed Moses to put his pale hand back into his garment and pull it back out. The color had returned to normal.

How Believable Are You as a Preacher?

The question many may have to wrestle with as we advance through this century is how believable is our message? Those who grew up in a church or were exposed to the church readily accept the gospel message. There was a time when biblical truths were taught and embraced at home and in the classrooms. Most of those in my generation and older grew up knowing simple things, such as the twenty-third Psalm or the Lord's Prayer. However, those days are long gone.

The evolution of handheld devices has changed the world, and it has challenged the message of the modern-day preacher. I remember the days of the Palm Pilot which may have been the beginning of this handheld revolution. We have gone from the Palm Pilot to the Blackberry, from flip phones to the newest smartphones on the market. As new devices are invented, those who are part of the older generation may be prone to ask the question: "What is that in your hand?"

What is in our hands has ushered in a new era. It used to be that the preacher carried in his or her hands a black book with the words *The Holy Bible* printed on its front leather cover. Those in my generation read, studied, believed, held sacred, and embraced the doctrines of the Bible. Regrettably, the inherent sacredness of sound Bible truths are no longer regularly taught nor readily accepted.

I am blessed to have five wonderful grandchildren. In addition, I am blessed to have them living close by and am able to see them frequently. Three of our grandchildren attend our church and enjoy sitting with their grandmother each Sunday. Like many in today's culture, my wife brings her iPad to church from which she reads her scripture. One Sunday she decided to use her traditional Bible rather than her iPad. My three-year-old granddaughter looked at her and asked, "G-Mom, what's that?"

The time has come when both children and adults may rarely see that once-familiar black book with the words *The Holy Bible* printed on the front, and on the inside, text in both black and red letters. This is the age of the handheld device.

In his book, *"Your Firm Everywhere Now: How to Position Your Professional Services Firm as an Authority in Your Marketplace, Increase Your Online Presence and Generate More Business,"* Michael Alf says "there are 7 billion people on the planet, there are 5.1 billion cell phones or mobile phones and only 4.2 billion toothbrushes. It clearly shows just how important handheld devices are today."[37] The amazing thing is "while most of these devices are cell phones, they are not used for just making phone calls. Thirty-nine percent (39%) of the cell phones are used to access the world wide web and other media interest." Of course, we do not need statistics to remind us of the abundance of these handheld devices. We see them all around us. It looks like everyone has at least one. It is amazing to see these devices in the hands of everyone between the cradle and the grave. I was nearly wiped off my feet the day my daughter forwarded me a picture of our nine-month-old granddaughter on the floor, using her finger to punch the screen of an electronic device.

Even though this is the generation of the handheld device, the preacher must never forget the importance of what is in his or her hand. Whether it is a book he can open and read from, or an electronic device where the words can be retrieved, the preacher has in his hand the eternal Word of God.

God Still Uses Preaching

It has been my honor over the past thirty years to have served as the under shepherd of Gethsemane Baptist Church in Newport News, Virginia. Sunday after Sunday, it has also been my responsibility to stand in the pulpit and deliver the weekly sermon. Looking back over the years, there have been few times, when I have sought to be faithful in preaching, that I have not seen someone come down the aisle in response to the worship experience and make a confession of faith or connect with the church. As a pastor and preacher, I admit that I am

---

[37] Michael Alf, *Your Firm Everywhere: How to Position Your Professional Services Firm as an Authority in Your Marketplace, Increase Your Online Presence and Generate More Business,* (Aspendale: Michael Alf/Totalu Pty Ltd. 2014), Kindle edition, loc 114.

often amazed at what happens after the sermon, i.e. the manner in which people respond to the gospel message. I can only affirm that God still uses preaching as his way of speaking to people and drawing them into a closer relationship with him. Dr. James Merritt says in his article, "Pastoral Leadership in a Postmodern World,"

> The biggest fear I have, in the way pastors and churches today are reacting to this whole concept of a postmodern world, is a loss of confidence in the Word of God. The Bible says about itself, in Hebrews 4, that "it is a two-edged sword." Either you believe that or not. If you believe that, then you have to agree with this: The Bible cuts whether you believe it will cut or not. You may be a postmodern who says 'I not only don't believe in absolute truth—it doesn't matter to me whether there's truth or not— that doesn't mean the truth will be ineffective. That doesn't mean the sword still will not cut.'[38]

I have experienced the impact and power of preaching in my own life. While I preach to others, like any preacher, there are times when I need to be preached to. There are times when preaching has had an impact on my life. One such instance that sticks out in my mind occurred several years ago when I was a seminary student. One of my fellow seminarians was killed at work by a gunman. I was deeply troubled by this incident. I found it hard to understand and deal with. I dealt with many questions and a wounded, restless spirit. However, as I sat in the pew at the funeral service, the words of the preacher were helpful and healing, and I came away feeling so much better than I'd felt before I arrived.

---

[38] Merritt, "Pastoral Leadership in a Postmodern World."

I suppose that the experiences of those who sit in the pews, listening to the preacher, is often much like that. Many may come in troubled and disturbed. However, God uses preaching to speak to mankind in unexplainable ways. One simply comes away knowing that there was a God encounter, and that something in them and about them has changed.

As I stand week after week preaching and teaching the gospel, I am often encouraged when members of the congregation and the community share with me how the message spoke to them and their situations, giving them hope, comfort, clarity, and confidence in God.

Even though we as preachers often wrestle with the relevance of our message, God continues to use our meager efforts to reach people in ways that we can hardly imagine. How many times has a sermon spoken to people we did not think we could reach in ways we never envisioned?

I am convinced that no matter the form, structure, or culture in which preaching takes place, God will still be God and will use the craft of preaching to accomplish his will in the lives of men, women, boys, and girls. This, however, does not negate the fact that the preacher must do his or her best to speak effectively to the needs of those who sit in the pews. It simply means that when the preacher does his or her best, the Holy Spirit will do the rest. My encouragement to the preacher is to keep on preaching, no matter the times or the challenges. Remember the charge that has been given to us through the words of the Apostle Paul in 2 Timothy 4:2 (KJV): "Preach the word; be instant in season, out of season."

Faith Comes by Hearing and Hearing the Word of God

Not long ago, I was watching the Dr. Oz Show and heard him promote a product that he said would help one lose a considerable amount of weight. Because the product was promoted by Dr. Oz, I ordered it and used it. I believed the product would do exactly what

Dr. Oz said it would do. I gained faith in the product because it had been promoted by a reliable source. If I had not heard of the product, I would not have been aware of it or of its benefits. Surely I would not have had faith in the product, because I wouldn't know that it existed.

In like manner, when a reliable person promotes God through preaching, the listener—who may not have known about God— suddenly becomes familiar with him. Based upon the preaching, the listener hears about God and then places his or her faith in God. Thus, the Apostle Paul says in Romans 10, "faith cometh by hearing."

Preaching, then, is necessary, as God uses preaching as the medium through which he draws others into a relationship with him. As I am writing these words, I reflect upon a conversation I had earlier today with one of my sisters. She shared with me how she had heard

> God uses preaching as the medium through which he draws others into a relationship with Him.

over and over the gospel message as it was preached to her. While she did not respond immediately, after hearing it more, she finally heard it as though for the first time. She believed, and her life has been transformed for the better. Though times have changed, it is quite evident that God has not changed his mind or his method when it comes to building faith. He uses preaching to draw a person to him for the first time, and he uses preaching as an ongoing medium through which he builds faith. Think of the many things you have come to believe because you have heard the preaching of the gospel. What God has done for you, he continues to do for others.

The Need for Explanation

The time in which we live is not simply the age of information. It's the age where information is accessible and available to anyone who looks for it. People can now access information from anywhere, on any subject; and they can do it without having to pay for it or can find a way to offset the cost. In some cases, the same information that is available to a preacher is also available to his audience. However, because the information is widely available and readily accessible does not negate the need for preaching the gospel.

The preacher in the twenty-first century might ask: What is the meaning and relevance of these handheld devices? The answer to that question underscores the fact that information is now in the hands of both the preacher and the people. But, just because information is available does not mean that individuals will invest the time to seek it. We all know that books and periodicals are available in bookstores and libraries around the world, but many of them have gone unread as depicted by a study from the Barna Group.

> The Barna Group conducted "The State of the Bible 2013" study for the American Bible Society, using 1,005 telephone interviews and 1,078 online surveys with a margin of error of the combined data of plus or minus 2 percentage points. The survey showed the Bible is still firmly rooted in American soil: 88 percent of respondents said they own a Bible, 80 percent think the Bible is sacred, 61 percent wish they read the Bible more, and the average household has 4.4 Bibles. The majority (57 percent) only read their Bibles four times a year or less. Only 26 percent of Americans said they read their Bible on a regular basis (four or more times a week).[39]

---

[39] Caleb K. Bell, "Poll: Americans Love the Bible but Don't Read It Much," *Religious News Service,* April 4, 2013, accessed February 20, 2015, http://www.religionnews.com/2013/04/04/poll-americans-love-the-bible-but-dont-read-it-much/.

The preacher spends considerable time bringing people information as well as inspiration that the average person may not seek out. In addition, the role of the preacher is far greater than that of providing information. The preacher is meant to bring to the people a "Word from the Lord." The Old Testament prophets always came to the people with the phrase, "thus saith the Lord." The preacher spends time in prayer, studying the scripture, and in the presence of the

> Preaching is not the idea or creativity of the preacher. It is the ingenuity of the Creator.

Lord, and comes away having heard from God. The preacher then stands before the people, declaring to them what the preacher has heard from God. The words on the pages of scripture become alive and find a place in the people's hearts, minds, and experiences.

The role of the preacher and preaching is significant since the preacher and preaching is God's chosen method for speaking to his people. The Apostle Paul declares "it pleased God by the foolishness of preaching to save them that believe" 1 Corinthians 1:21 (KJV): Preaching is not the idea or creativity of the preacher. It is the ingenuity of the Creator. God in his providence decided to use preaching to prick the hearts of people with his message. God calls and chooses whom he desires to be the instrument to disseminate his Word. Therefore, the importance and the need for preaching the gospel transcends time, cultural shifts, and changes in communication, as well as the availability of information. No matter the times or challenges that the preacher may face, the gospel must be preached.

In addition, the availability of information to the world does not negate the need for preaching. The words of scripture must be spiritually discerned. The Apostle Paul says, "But the natural man receiveth not the things of the Spirit of God: for they are foolishness unto him: neither can he know them because they are spiritually discerned." 2 Corinthians 2:14 (KJV). On the one hand, the preacher sits in the presence of God, seeking to hear and know what God is saying to his people. On the other hand, the preacher stands before the people to explain what God is saying.

In Acts chapter 8, an Ethiopian eunuch who served in the royal court of Queen Candice was sitting in the chariot after attending a worship service. While he sat there, he was reading from the prophet Isaiah. Since he had just returned from worship, he may have been reflecting on something he had heard that day in the temple or a passage of scripture might have caught his attention for one reason or another. Given his lofty role and position in the queen's court, one might assume that his academic background would have equipped him to comprehend and understand what he was reading. However, the Spirit of God, speaking through an angel, directed Phillip to join the eunuch at his chariot. When Phillip arrived, he asked him a simple question: "Do you understand what you are reading?" The eunuch responded by saying, "How can I, except some man should guide me?" (Acts 8:31 KJV). The eunuch acknowledged that the scriptures were different from other books and writings. The correct explanation of the scripture does not come from the classroom, off a flat-screen TV, or from the lips of a professor. Rather, someone who is spiritual must explain the spiritual truth of scripture.

The times in which we live are no different from the times of the eunuch. Though we live in a well-informed culture, the need for explaining scriptures is as crucial today as it was then. In an article by Mark Kelly entitled, "Study: Unchurched Americans Turned Off by Church, Open to Christians," Kelly comments on research conducted by LifeWay Research—which is a research arm of LifeWay Christian Resources—and the North American Mission Board. He says, "the survey found that many unchurched people do not have a biblical understanding of God and Jesus."[40] Clearly people need someone who is capable of helping them understand spiritual truths as recorded in scripture. There are still those who want to know what God is saying and how the Bible applies to their lives. I am convinced that those who are caught up in the hustle and bustle of this busy world are still trying to find meaning in life, and they will only do so as they come to understand the words of scripture. The preacher who is called and anointed by God is uniquely qualified to explain the scripture. Preachers are able to do so because they spend more time than most reading, studying and plowing through scripture and finding meaning for themselves and others. While some may reject the word of God, preachers must not lose hope and hang up their robes and put away their Bibles. As God said to the prophet Elijah, he had seven thousand who had not bowed to Baal.

A Changing Culture and an Open Door

I am convinced that God has set before the church an open door. The opportunity for sharing the gospel message is as great today as it has ever been. Every age and generation has had its challenges and cultural shifts, and the gospel has been effective in each generation. The preacher, however, must seek to discover and find effective ways of reaching the people to whom he or she has been called to minister. This may mean that the preacher has to spend time understanding the culture and the context in which he or she has been called to serve. There are numerous resources that are available and can assist the preacher.

---

[40] Mark Kelly, "Study: Unchurched Americans Turned Off by Church, Open to Christians," Lifeway Research, January 9, 2008, accessed February 20, 2015, http://www.lifeway.com/Article/LifeWay-Research-finds-unchurched-Americans-turned-off-by-church-open-to-Christians

In addition to print and other media resources, the preacher might consider utilizing a team approach to sermon preparation. The preacher may discover the value of others' input regarding the content of a sermon. This might be a stretch for some, but it will be a good stretch. The familiar cliché that two heads are better than one is also applicable to preaching. Oftentimes, after preaching a sermon, I think of so many things I should have said. What if some of those thoughts had been suggested to me prior to my delivering the sermon? The prophet Ezekiel was said to have joined the community in exile, sitting where they sat. As a part of the doctor of ministry in preaching program through the Association of Chicago Theological Seminary, students are required to use a parish project group. The parish project group serves as a resource to help the preacher identify relevant issues among the congregation. Making use of a parish group or any other group allows the preacher to sit where the people sit and to better understand the ways in which the people are challenged. The preacher then connects the Word of God to those matters.

The same question that God asked Moses may then be the same question the twenty-first century preacher is being asked today: "What is in thine hand?" Many years ago, I attended the Hampton University Minister's Conference. The setting was in Ogden Hall, the preacher was the late Reverend Doctor A. Lewis Patterson of Houston, Texas. Dr. Patterson said to us, "You are the only one standing, so preach awhile." Preachers, you have what you need in your hand. Why not allow it to lead you into a promising future of preaching?

Questions for Discussion and Reflection:

1. When you heard God's call, did you feel adequate?
2. How has God developed you over the years? What lessons have you learned? What tools have you gained? In what ways are you seeking to build upon those lessons?

3. Do you believe that the Bible is still relevant and that its words have the power to transform the lives of people in this century?

4. How do you feel about discussing your sermon with members of your congregation or some other group for the purpose of assisting in sermon development?

5. Would you consider using such a group in the future?

CHAPTER EIGHT

PREACHING TO A
MULTIGENERATIONAL CONGREGATION

On the first day of the week, when we met to
break bread, Paul was holding a discussion with them;
since he intended to leave the next day, he continued
speaking until midnight. 8 There were many lamps in
the room upstairs where we were meeting. 9 A young
man named Eutychus, who was sitting in the window,
began to sink off into a deep sleep while Paul talked
still longer. Overcome by sleep, he fell to the ground
three floors below and was picked up dead.

—Acts 20:7–9 NRSB

Almost every preacher at one time or another has had the unpleasant experience of someone falling asleep during the sermon. The Apostle Paul, who is known for many things and especially for great preaching, was no exception. The story recorded in Acts 20 tells that Paul had gathered a great crowd. Because of the demands of his schedule, he preached way into the night so that he could travel the next day. The experience of Paul and others in this story are relevant to the future of preaching.

If we examine the story to gather helpful insight regarding the future of preaching, we are able to observe the best practices when it comes to preaching. Preachers who enjoy good preaching along with reading and listening to the sermons of others may find it helpful to talk with other preachers regarding the effectiveness of their sermon. Questions may be raised, such as what makes a sermon work. How does one measure the effectiveness of a sermon? What are some of the key things to keep in mind when developing and delivering a sermon? This story has a lot to offer in this regard.

It is the first day of the week. According to the calendar, it was a Sunday when those who celebrated the resurrection of Jesus gathered. The time of day is not given. I would suppose it must have been around eleven in the morning. That is the time when most churches in our culture hold services.

Without question, this must have been a traditional gathering. The text referenced "when the disciples came together to break bread." Coming together to break bread was becoming an established tradition in the early church. The disciples "met from house to house, eating and breaking bread with singleness of heart." Perhaps someone was scheduled to deliver the message that day, but yielded to the guest preacher in the house. After all, it was an honor for the disciples to have Paul in their midst. There are people of faith who are treated with such respect and reverence, agendas are placed on hold so that their voices can be heard. Once the word was out that Paul was in town and would be speaking, the crowd must have increased. From all indications, Paul found himself preaching to a multigenerational crowd. Certainly there were those in the crowd from Paul's own age group, men and women who were well established in their careers and home lives. A man by the name of Eutychus was also there. The King James translation refers to Eutychus as a young man, which means he was between the ages of twenty-five and forty. This would mean Eutychus was not brought to the worship service by a parent. He was old enough to make decisions on his own. Perhaps he had heard of Paul and decided to gather with the other disciples.

Preachers of all ages have preached to multigenerational congregations. While the average pastor attracts individuals that are his or her peers, most congregations are comprised of various age groups. Some congregations will have more of one age group than another. Surveying the demographics of the church will often assist the pastor in better reaching his or her congregation. In addition, observing the trends of churches' demographics may be helpful in predicting the future of a congregation. On the website marketingteacher.com, in a post dated May 8, 2014, by Tim Friesner, Dr. Jill Novak of the University of Phoenix and Texas A&M University says, that "in America, there are six living generations, which are six fairly distinct groups of people. As a generalization, each generation has different likes, dislikes, and attributes."[41]

According to the article, there are the

- GI generation, born 1901–1926
- Mature/silents, born 1927–1945
- Baby boomers, born between 1946 and 1964
- Generation X, born between 1965 and 1980

---

[41] Tim Friesner, "The Six Living Generations in America," May 8, 2014, accessed April 8, 2015, http://www.marketingteacher.com/the-six-living-generations-in-america/

- Generation Y/millennium, born between 1981 and 2000
- Generation Z/boomlets, born after 2001

Your personal research will help you to understand the characteristics of each of these groups.

I have always been under the impression that I know the congregation I serve very well. To my surprise, a recent survey of the congregation through a simple report from the church's data bank was quite revealing. Needless to say, the guesswork of knowing who was in the pews was removed. In addition, the picture regarding the cross sections of the congregation is much clearer.

As the preacher understands the demographics of his or her audience, it then becomes necessary to understand the characteristics of those demographics. Apparently, Paul had not thought too deeply concerning his audience. He experienced what every preacher has experienced—someone in his audience went to sleep while he was preaching.

The Multigenerational Sermon

Given the range of ages and experiences, as well as likes and dislikes, of a congregation, a preacher's sermon cannot be a flat-screen presentation, but should be a 3-D experience. When I refer to a flat screen, I mean a sermon that will only resonate with one group in an audience. A sermon must be three- or even six-dimensional. The preacher must think, speak, and deliver the sermon in a multidimensional manner. This may require the preacher to step outside of his or her own comfort zone and explore with the sermon. The sermon may need language and images from various generations. While each preacher is a product of his or her own era, it is wise to become familiar with the culture of each age group represented in the congregation. Becoming familiar with an age group can be as simple as becoming acquainted with someone in each age group. Through those relationships, the preacher will be able to gather information and develop insight.

I have referenced the parish project group that I work with in the ACT doctor of ministry preaching program. In that group, I intentionally include individuals from various generations. Once, I was working on a sermon about Joseph and what his coat of many colors must have looked like. In an attempt to make the sermon relevant to today, I talked with a few people in the group who were around the same age as Joseph. They helped me understand not only the style of clothes they wore, but the language and experiences of their age group. As I used some of their language and referred to things in their world during the sermon, they paid close attention. The future of preaching requires the preacher to work harder to make those connections and seek ways to engage his or her audience.

Deliver the Sermon from Boredom

A deacon in my church once said, "No one wants to hear a dead, dry sermon." Of course, the terms *dead* and *dry* need to be defined. One way to define them is with the word *boring*. With the arrival of computer-generated images, digital sound, and cell phone cameras that produce high-quality pictures, it does not take much for people to get bored. Preachers have stiff competition when delivering their message. Many congregants bring their cell phones and tablets to worship; and while the preacher is preaching, they're paying closer attention to their electronic devices. They are reading text messages and e-mails; they're tweeting and talking on Facebook. With all of these distractions occurring, the preacher must keep his audience's attention and keep his audience engaged. Some are making use of video screens, creative backdrops, and are even including the congregants' devices as part of the sermon. Sermons must be colorful and creative, and their content must be impactful and captivating. Clearly, I am not suggesting that the preacher resort to gimmicks. However, there is no limitation on the amount of creativity that can be used to make the message effective.

When God wanted Jeremiah to understand how he could reshape Israel into the image God desired, he sent Jeremiah to the potter's house to observe the potter working on his wheel. When God wanted Peter to take the gospel to the Gentile world, he unveiled a knit sheet before Peter's eyes with images of all kinds of animals on it. When Jesus wanted to teach Peter a message on evangelism, he took him out in a boat and told him where to cast his net for a great catch. He then said that Peter would now catch men. Creativity in sermon delivery may help to deliver the sermon from boredom.

How Long Should the Sermon Last?

How long should the sermon last? This is a question the Apostle Paul probably should have asked. He preached way into the night in Troas. Surely, had he been preaching in the average pulpit today, he would have been preaching all by himself. He preached so long, Eutychus not only fell asleep, he fell out the window and to his death. If there was ever a case of someone who was preached to death, this was certainly the one. Beyond Paul's ability to capture and hold the attention of his audience, he was long-winded. The challenge for many preachers is something called brevity. So often, there is so much to say and so little time in which to say it.

However, the preacher is facing an even greater challenge when delivering a sermon. In addition to digital sounds and sights that capture the attention of almost everyone, life now happens at such a rapid pace. There is an increased focus on speed. As a result, the attention span of the average person is decreasing. "According to the National Center for Biotechnology Information, at the U.S.

Goldfish have an attention span of 9 seconds — 1 second more than you.

National Library of Medicine, the average attention span of a human being has dropped from 12 seconds in 2000 to 8 seconds in 2013. This is one second less than the attention span of a goldfish. That's right, goldfish have an attention span of 9 seconds—1 second more than you."[42]

Given these facts, it may mean that if the preacher is still preaching the same length sermon today that he or she was preaching fifteen years ago, his audience has checked out before the sermon makes its landing. By no means am I suggesting that the length of a sermon must be reduced to coincide with these statistics. That would mean that, over time, the sermon may be reduced to nothing. However, it does suggest that the length of the sermon should be taken into consideration. There are various schools of thought on how long a sermon should be. Few may agree upon whether there should be any set period of time. Every preacher should know his or her audience and govern the sermon's length accordingly.

The Sermon Must Become Incarnational

Even though Paul presented a long sermon, he knew when it was time for the sermon to end and for him to plunge into action. The moment Eutychus fell out of the window, Paul ended his sermon and immediately ran outside to Eutychus's body. He could have assigned others to look after the young man, but, Paul went outside himself to see about Eutychus and to access his condition. Paul fell on him, embraced him, and waited until life had returned. He could have prayed for the young man from a distance, but he did not. He joined

---

[42] Michael Brenner, "Thanks Social Media—Our Average Attention Span is Now Shorter than Goldfish," Sap Business Innovation, May 30, 2014, accessed February 24, 2015, Blogs.sap.com/innovation/sales-marketing/thanks-social-media-average-attention-span-now-shorter-goldfish-01251966.

him in his condition. He knew when it was time to preach and when it was time to practice what he preached.

Preaching in the future must be incarnational. Preachers may have to leave the safety and comfort of the pulpit and sanctuary and join people where they are, sharing in their plights and desperate conditions. The message has to come to life by meeting people in their moments of difficulty and distress. After all, the gospel message is the proclamation of one who took on the human condition. Chapter 1 of the Gospel of St. John declares that the Word became flesh and dwelt among us. The Christ that is proclaimed in the gospels was not untouchable or far removed from those to whom he preached. As a preacher, Jesus often found his pulpit outside of the synagogue or temple. He went to where the people were and proclaimed the Word, demonstrating his love, care, and concern for the masses. When his disciples would have dismissed the crowd and sent them home, he allowed the crowd to remain and fed them. When a group following him in the streets would have silenced a blind beggar, Jesus called the blind man to his side and opened his eyes. When a widow was on her way to the graveyard to bury her only son, Jesus touched the coffin and caused the child to be raised. He is Emanuel, God who is with us. He cared enough to stop being the Word and to come into our world. We who preach this gospel may have to divest ourselves of our vestments and put on the clothes of human suffering in order to proclaim that the gospel we preach is believable and livable.

Questions for Discussion and Reflection:

1. How well do you understand the characteristics of the six generations in the church today?

2. Have you ever been bored by a sermon; and if so, what did it feel like to you?

3. What do you do to keep your sermons interesting and exciting?

4. How comfortable are you with trying something creative in preaching to increase the effectiveness of your sermon?

5. How long are your sermons, and would your congregation say you preach too long, too short, or just right?

6. In what ways does your preaching speak to the life experiences of your audience?

CHAPTER NINE

PREACHING EVERYWHERE

And they went out and proclaimed the good news everywhere, while the Lord worked with them and confirmed the message by the signs that accompanied it.
—Mark 16:20 NRSV

The disciples of Jesus took their charge to preach the good news of the gospel seriously. They were faithful in carrying out their assignment, which was to "go into all the world." The concluding chapter of Mark's gospel suggests that the disciples "preached everywhere." The term everywhere may seem exhaustive, yet it is clearly understood that the disciples were limited to carrying the gospel throughout the Roman Empire and the known Gentile world. Everywhere referred to everywhere the disciples had the ability to travel to.

Every era has its own everywhere. As the ability to travel and communicate has expanded throughout the centuries, so has the span of everywhere. Certainly, everywhere today has a far greater reach than it has had at any other time in history. Given the advancements in technology and social media, there are few places that are off limits for preaching the gospel. In the times in which we live, the gospel can literally go almost everywhere—into almost every continent, country, and culture.

A door has been set open before the twenty-first century preacher. Opportunities to share the gospel are as great today as they have ever been. Preaching everywhere can be easily accomplished through social media. Social media has not only made it possible to carry the gospel everywhere, it has made it practical to do so.

Preachers no longer have to wait for an invitation or opportunity to preach the gospel. They need only take advantage of the many opportunities at their doorsteps. These opportunities to preach everywhere are also reminders that the church has always been called and commissioned to go. This is an important reminder that people only show up in the pews after the church has responded to the Great Commission, which is the command to "go into all the world." When thinking of the future of preaching, we must look closely at the many ways preachers can take the gospel everywhere through the use of social media.

What is social media? It is the medium through which people can connect, share, and communicate digitally. The digital world has opened up so many new possibilities that allow people to connect and access information. Some may remember the days of the telephone book, with it white pages for residential phone numbers and the yellow pages for business information. Most of us relied upon newspapers, magazines, and encyclopedias as sources of information. While these sources still exist, they are overshadowed by the Internet's ability to deliver even more information almost instantly.

Today, social media has become the primary source of information for many people. Name it and you can locate it on the Internet. In the same way that information can be gathered via the Internet and social media, information can also be shared. Social media gives everyone a voice, opinion, and perspective. So much so, a person's credibility and survival can come to depend on what others write or say about them on the social media.

Social media can be a meaningful tool for preaching the gospel and for evangelism. It has the ability to engage the unchurched and nonbelievers in conversations in a nonintrusive manner, with people they trust or with whom they have a relationship. It also allows one to carry the message of Jesus to believers who might not be able to travel to your physical location, but are still seeking to learn more about Christ.

If Jesus Were Living among us Today, Would He use Social Media?

On the outer doors to sanctuaries, I've seen signs that say Turn Off Your Cell Phone. The cell phone and other electronic devices can be viewed as instruments that should never be used in the sanctuary. Given the depth with which cell phones and other electronic devices have become a part of our culture, I wonder if Jesus—were he alive and living among us—would he insist on the use of social media. To answer, we can look at the time when he healed the blind men in a house. He specifically told them not to tell anyone; however, they went out and told everybody what he had done for them. They used the social media of their day. In many cases, crowds came out to see Jesus because they'd heard what others said about him. His fame and reputation spread because people were always talking about the good things he did for them.

If those who experienced his power at work in their lives had remained silent, chances are his audiences would not have been as large as they were. However, once the word got out about him, because of the witnesses going viral and spreading the news, people from all walks of life came from everywhere to see him. Crowds were pushing and rushing in the streets, traveling along the seashores, climbing trees, and staying late into the night, all because his fame spread throughout the land. As the modern-day preacher seeks to share the gospel message, the question must be raised: How are people hearing about Jesus? We may even consider asking how people are hearing about preachers today. What's being socially said about the preacher and his or her message? This survey cannot be limited to those in the pews. It must be taken by polling people everywhere, because people everywhere are on social media.

What Appears When Your Name is Googled?

Most people use the Internet as their primary resource to investigate and garner information related to commerce, travel, news, activities, and faith. On Google, the third most searched content, behind pornography and dating, is *faith*. When someone goes online searching for matters of faith, will your name appear? When a person has a presence on the World Wide Web, with a website or a blog, they are automatically given credibility. About eleven years ago, this paradigm shifted with the introduction of social media. Social media offers people seeking information a deeper perspective and understanding of what they are looking for, based on the opinions of others. For the first time, a multiconversational platform is also available.

Social media gives instant access and credibility to your ministry brand. Many people that are searching for churches, worship services, and ministries no longer have to physically go to a building. They rely on social media sites to engage in conversations, view videos, and hear messages that available on the Internet. Social media offers the opportunity to connect your message to a global virtual world, whether through downloading digital content such as video, manuscript text documents, or audio files. The ability to research and connect with you is instantaneous, while simultaneously allowing each social media visitor to communicate back to you.

You will never know exactly who everyone is that is researching or viewing your information. However, through continued posts, one can build virtual relationships. Social media, therefore, allows a person or ministry to build a virtual following of individuals they may never see. Once popularity and credibility grows, so will the audience.

In addition, other ways to share the gospel message are through live streaming, on-demand services, podcasting, and blogging, all of which are a result of the evolution of digital communication. A ministry can now be a megaministry online with a huge following, and a smaller physical, local congregation. Several years ago, a preacher friend had a congregation that was not as large as he desired. He started broadcasting his worship services over the radio. He told me it helped to know that when he preached, he was actually preaching to a much larger crowd because hundreds were listening to him over the radio. The same can be said about live streaming a sermon, or allowing the sermon to be offered on-demand in audio or video format. The preacher is preaching to an audience that is far larger than those sitting in the pews. An Internet and social media presence also opens endless opportunities for e-commerce, tithers, donations, and other valuable marketplace opportunities that will help support the local ministry.

Make a First Impression Online

Social media may be equated to a parking lot ministry, greeters, or the ushers that greet visitors or members of a church. Most people will initially research you and your church online to gain basic information about you to help them make decisions about visiting. Given the swiftness of the Internet, you have only a short period of time to capture the attention of potential followers. Serious attention should be given to one's webpage or other social medial setups. The information should be creative and captivating. Your online presence should be updated regularly and reviewed, as changes are constantly taking place. If your goal is to reach people everywhere and connect the gospel to the unchurched, social media has to be a priority.

The Twenty-First Century Preacher Must Embrace Social Media

An area of training and development for the twenty-first century preacher is the use of social media for ministry. In the same way that professionals such as doctors, dentists, and educators are trained in using new equipment and tools, the preacher must also be trained to use new tools. Modern technology is certainly one of those tools. Rob O'Lynn, in a July 2014 article titled, "Social Media and Preaching: A Primer," suggests that there are three levels or categories of media experts.

> Digital natives are people who use technology fluidly ... Digital immigrants are people who use technology although not fluidly ... Digital aliens are people who do not use technology unless it is

> absolutely necessary (i.e., email for work, text-messaging only with select people). Each of us falls into one of these categories. That's the bad news, especially for those who believe that rotary phones are on the comeback.[43]

It really does not matter what category a person is in. The possibility of launching a digitally based ministry is high, given the ease, abundance, and availability of media devices and applications. Remember that practice makes perfect. The more you use something, the more you learn about it and the more familiar you will become with it. And while you are learning to use social media, one of the greatest resources to help you is right at your fingertips. Most of us are surrounded by young people, in our families, churches, or community who are familiar with social media and are willing to offer their skills. In recruiting them, a preacher not only creates an effective social media presence, but also brings value to and develops a new ministry for a generation that has often been neglected by local assemblies.

Social Media is Affordable

Social media allows for instant global reach and unlimited resources with limited investment. A church, no matter its size, will find that the playing field is based on one's commitment to the tool. The infrastructure of social media allows the megachurch and the small church to have the exact same opportunity based on infrastructure. The deciding factor of potential impact is based on your commitment to maximizing the opportunity of this tool. For minimal investment, your entire brand can be global. Social media

---

[43] Rob O'Lynn, "Social Media and Preaching: A Primer (Part One of Two)," Working Preacher, July 1, 2014, accessed February 24, 2015, https://www.workingpreacher.org/craft.aspx?post=3267.

is a free marketing tool that allows your congregants, friends, and family members to market for you, based on their experiences and interactions with you. No longer is there a need for radio, television, a huge IT staff, or marketing budgets. Social media is readily available to take you global, with no boundaries or restraints.

Social Media and the Preacher

In today's culture, preaching should not only take place in a physical building or within the four walls of the church. A preacher has to go where the people are. For generations, preaching has been focused on getting people into the buildings via local outreach initiatives, marketing, programs, and word of mouth. Today, preachers and churches that do not have a social media presence will not grow because the ascendant culture is communicating online. If a preacher desires to grow his or her ministry in the twenty-first century, social media has to be an intricate part of the initiatives. The social media has to be focused on communication between the layperson and the actual community within the church and without. There is no more separation between church members and members of the local community. Social media affords the preacher the ability to be global and to build virtually, while connecting his or her message to people who may never set foot in the actual church. The goal in using social media to go everywhere is to embrace those who have decided it is not necessary to travel from their homes to the church. Social media eliminates the miles of travel and places the gospel message wherever a person may be. Many times, the person who needs to hear the message most is only a social media post away. If the preacher is going to be serious about getting out the message, he or she must also be serious about establishing alternative assembly locations. One of the assembling locations can be online where people are consistently social.

The twenty-first century preacher can now seize the moment, get online, and go places he or she would not otherwise go. As social media is the wave of the future, it provides a great tool for the preacher to fulfill the assignment to "go into the all the world."

Questions for Discussion and Reflection:

1. In what ways have you used social media to expand your reach in preaching the gospel?

2. When your name is Googled, what information surfaces about you?

3. What new areas of social media would you like to implement in your ministry and how do you plan to go about it?

4. What level of expertise do you have in social media: digital native, digital immigrant, or digital alien?

5. Who do you know that could help you take your ministry to the next level by using social media?

CHAPTER TEN

PREACH WITH BOLDNESS

And now, Lord, look at their threats, and grant to your servants to speak your word with all boldness while you stretch out your hand to heal, and signs and wonders are performed through the name of your holy servant[b] Jesus. When they had prayed, the place in which they were gathered together was shaken; and they were all filled with the Holy Spirit and spoke the word of God with boldness.

—Acts 4:29–32 NRSV

This book has only touched the tip of the iceberg regarding the conversations that must take place about preaching in the future. Only a few ideas and concepts have been addressed. It is my aim that this is a beginning point, a pilot light that will get the discussion going. Given all that has been shared, I have an additional comment. Without regard to the preacher's thoughts on the future of preaching, there is one thing for sure: the twenty-first century preacher must preach like never before with boldness and confidence.

People want to know that the message the preacher preaches is one he or she stands by, no matter how it may be received. Preachers are not effective if they waver, or if they are unclear or uncertain about what they believe and preach. Going forward, the preacher must preach with boldness.

First-century preachers faced a time of shifts, transitions, and uncertainty, and they preached with boldness. The story recorded in Acts chapter 4 is a great example.

Peter and John had been recently released from jail. Preaching Jesus had been no picnic or summer vacation for them. They had been arrested, handcuffed, and then later released after receiving a smack on the wrist and a threat from the judge that if they ever showed up in his courtroom again, the consequences would be dire. Like their Lord, they were jailed and brought to court on charges that could not stick in anyone's court of law. They were not guilty of any sex crime, grand larceny, or any other crime of that nature. They had not harmed anyone or taken anything from anyone. In fact, they had done quite the opposite.

Peter and John had been on their way to a prayer meeting, when they encountered a man who was lame and soliciting alms. Previously, the two disciples had been filled with the Holy Spirit (Acts 2). They were now stewards of the power of God and were ready to empower others who were in need. They knew they had been given this power to be a witness to the resurrections of Jesus. God would validate them by working miracles through them. They did not have to go looking for some place or a group of people before whom they would perform these miracles. They would not have to hold a tent revival to draw people to them, nor make up flyers to pass out or post signs on windows. They didn't have to post an announcement on Facebook or Instagram, or do any other kind of marketing regarding their new power. They were just to go about their daily routine. And so they came upon a man who was lame, helpless, and desiring only crumbs, or a penny or two. While there is a place for marketing and announcing one's programs and ministries, sometimes the Lord uses his people and draws his own crowd.

When the lame man asked them for money, Peter uttered his famous line: "Silver and gold have I none but such as I have given I thee, in the name of Jesus of Christ of Nazareth, rise up and walk" (Acts 3:6 KJV).

At Peter's command, the man stood and started walking. It was not long before the word got out, and Peter and John were credited with the miracle. The authorities showed up—the fire marshals, the codes and compliance officers, and law enforcement. Peter and John had not applied for a special-use permit, a license to conduct a public service, or received permission from the authorities to perform miracles. So the authorities shut down their storefront movement and arrested them.

After they had harassed and threatened Peter and John, the authorities told them to stop preaching about Jesus or even use his name. If they were going to preach, then they needed to go to their schools and learn to preach the way the Pharisees preached. "Don't bring that new stuff up around here," the disciples were told. "Don't preach another gospel."

Peter and John responded by continuing to preach. Given the dire situation they faced, they preached with boldness. Given all that is taking place in our world today, there is a need now for bold preaching.

What is bold preaching? Bold preaching is preaching that stands out. While the preacher must live in and minister and preach to a world that is changing, he or she must have a gospel that stands out. When people experience critical moments in their lives, they look for something that is different, something that is meaningful. The gospel does not have to blend in to be effective. It can stand out and be embraced.

Bold preaching is preaching that sets a standard. In a time when anything goes, the preacher must raise the standard. The gospel does not have to be watered down in order to flow into the lives of people. It must set a standard and call people to rise to that standard. The preacher must be willing to declare that standard and to live by it without fear or shame.

Bold preaching is the preaching of the good news that is worth spreading. The disciples did not stay in one place. They went everywhere, spreading the good news. The times in which we live demand that the gospel message be spread like never before. Today's preacher must seek ways to spread that message. While much of our world today seeks cutbacks and reductions, the preacher is on a quest to shout his or her message from the rooftops.

My prayer is that all preachers will preach with boldness. In so doing, the future will embrace preaching as valuable and necessary. Preach, preacher, for preaching indeed has a future.

BIBLIOGRAPHY

Alf, Michael. *Your Firm Everywhere: How to Position Your Professional Services Firm as an Authority in Your Marketplace, Increase Your Online Presence and Generate More Business.* Aspendale: Michael Alf/Totalu Pty Ltd., 2014.

Anderson, Kenton. "The Future of Preaching." accessed January 29, 2015, http://www.preaching.org/futureofhomiletics/.

Avery, Richard K., and Don Marsh. *Soaring Where Christ Has Led: Innovative Worship Ideas for the 21*st *Century.* Lima, OH: CSS Pub., 2002.

Barna, George, and David Kinnaman. *Churchless: Understanding Today's Unchurched and How to Connect with Them.* Austin, TX: Tyndale House Publishers, Inc., 2014.

Bell, Caleb K. *Poll: Americans Love the Bible but Don't Read It Much,* Religious News Service, April 4, 2013. http://www.religionnews.com/2013/04/04/poll-americans-love-the-bible-but-dont-read-it-much/.

Brenner, Michael. "Thanks Social Media—Our Average Attention Span is Now Shorter than Goldfish," Sap Business Innovation. May 30, 2014, Blogs.sap.com/innovation/sales-marketing/thanks-social-media-average-attention-span-now-shorter-goldfish-01251966.

Bundschuh, Rick. *Don't Rock the Boat, Capsize It: Loving the Church Too Much to Leave It the Way It Is.* Colorado Springs: NavPress, 2005.

Carroll, Jim. *The Future Belongs to Those Who Are Fast: The Best of the Insight from JimCarroll.com.* Mississauga, Ontario: Oblio Press, 2012.

Chapman, Steven Curtis, and Scotty Smith. *Restoring Broken Things: What Happens When We Catch a Vision for the New World Jesus Is Creating.* Nashville: Integrity Publishers, 2005.

Cosgrove, Charles H., and Herold Weiss. *Cross-Cultural Paul: Journeys to Others, Journeys to Ourselves.* Grand Rapids, MI: W. B. Eerdmans Pub., 2005.

Cosgrove, Charles H., and W. Dow Edgerton. *In Other Words: Incarnational Translation for Preaching.* Grand Rapids, MI: W. B. Eerdmans Pub., 2007.

Dally, John Addison. *Choosing the Kingdom: Missional Preaching for the Household of God(Vital Worship Healthy Congregations).* Herndon, VA: Alban Institute, 2007.

Duduit, Michael. *Conversations on Preaching.* Franklin, TN: Preaching Press, 2004.

Friesner, Tim. "The Six Living Generations in America." MarketingTeacher.com. May 8, 2014. http://www.marketingteacher. com/the-six-living-generations-in-america/.

Gibson, Scott M. *Preaching to a Shifting Culture: 12 Perspectives on Communicating That Connects.* Grand Rapids, MI: Baker Books, 2004.

Hearon, Holly E. *The Bible in Ancient and Modern Media: Story and Performance.* Eugene, OR: Cascade Books, 2009.

Hughes, R. Kent. *Preach the Word: Essays on Expository Preaching in Honor of R. Kent Hughes.* Wheaton, IL: Crossway Books, 2007.

Jones, Peyton. "Preaching to the Postmodern Generation," accessed April 7, 2015. http://www.gospel-preaching.com/resources/ Preaching%20To%20The%20Postmodern%20Generation.pdf.

Johnston, Graham. *Preaching to a Postmodern World: A Guide to Reaching Twenty-first Century Listeners.* Grand Rapids, MI: Baker Books, 2001.

Kelly, Mark. "Study: Unchurched Americans Turned Off by Church, Open to Christians." Lifeway Research. January 9, 2008. http://www.lifeway.com/Article/LifeWay-Research-finds-unchurched-Americans-turned-off-by-church-open-to-Christians.

King, Clayton. "*Rethinking Preaching: Whatever It Takes to Make the Gospel Clear,* Facts & Trends. April 28, 2014. factsandtrends. net/2014/04/28/rethinking-preaching-whatever-it-takes-to-make-the-gospel-clear/#.VPSq_PnF-sSo.

Libronix Digital Library System. "Acts: Unlocking the Scriptures for You." [Computer File], electronic ed. Cincinnati, OH: Standard, 1987.

Long, Jimmy. *The Leadership Jump: Building Partnerships between Existing and Emerging Christian Leaders.* Downers Grove, IL: IVP Books, 2009.

Merritt, James "Pastoral Leadership in a Postmodern World." February 2003. www.uu.edu/centers/rglee/fellows/fall03/ merritt.htm.

McGuinness, Mark. *Resilience: Facing down Rejection & Criticism on the Road to Success.* Lateral Action Books, 2012.

O'Lynn, Rob. "Social Media and Preaching: A Primer (Part One of Two)." Working Preacher, July 1, 2014. https://www. workingpreacher.org/craft.aspx?post=3267.

Olson, David T. *The American Church in Crisis: Groundbreaking Research Based on a National Database of over 200,000 Churches.* Grand Rapids, MI: Zondervan, 2008.

Pope, Randy, and Randy Pope. *The Intentional Church: Moving from Church Success to Community Transformation.* rev. ed. Chicago: Moody Publishers, 2006.

Rainer, Thom S. *Autopsy of a Deceased Church: 12 Ways to Keep Yours Alive.* Nashville: B&H Publishing Group, 2014.

Relevant Preaching. "Preaching, Leading the Church, Proclaiming the Word." July 25, 2010. http://www.preaching.com/resources/articles/11653970/.

Seacombe, Mark. "Going Forward let's consign this insane phrase to history." *The Guardian.* August 30, 2011. http://www. theguardian.com/media/mind-your-language/2011/aug/30/mind-your-language-going-forward.

Scott, Susan. *Fierce Conversations: Achieving Success at Work & in Life, One Conversation at a Time.* New York: Viking, 2002.

Sjogren, Steve. *101 Ways to Reach Your Community.* Colorado Springs: NavPress, 2001.

Smith, William. *Smith's Bible Dictionary.* 1901 ed. Biblestudy.com.

Stevenson, Geoffrey. *The Future of Preaching*. Norwich, England: SCM Press, 2010.

Stott, John R. W. *Between Two Worlds: The Art of Preaching in the Twentieth Century*. Grand Rapids, MI: W. B. Eerdmans, 1982.

Thomas, Frank. *They Like to Never Quit Praising God: The Role of Celebration in Preaching*. Cleveland: The Pilgrim Press, 2013.

Veith, Gene Edward. *Postmodern Times: A Christian Guide to Contemporary Thought and Culture*. Wheaton, IL: Crossway Books, 1994.

Waltz, Mark L. *First Impressions: Creating Wow Experiences in Your Church*. Loveland, CO: Group Pub., 2005.

Whitman, Matt. *Putting God in His Place: Exalting God in the iCulture*. Minneapolis: Next Step Resources, 2011.

Willimon, William H. *Conversations with Barth on Preaching*. Nashville: Abingdon Press, 2006.

Wilson, Paul Scott. *The Four Pages of the Sermon: A Guide to Biblical Preaching*. Nashville: Abingdon Press, 1999.

Printed in the United States
By Bookmasters